NEURO-MASTERY

Neuro-Mastery
Unlocking Your Brain's Potential for Lasting Success

Dr. Pamela Seraphine

©2024 All Rights Reserved. No portion of this book may be reproduced, stored in a retrieval system, or transmitted in any form or by any means—electronic, mechanical, photocopy, recording, scanning, or other—except for brief quotations in critical reviews or articles without the prior permission of the author.

Published by Game Changer Publishing

Paperback ISBN: 978-1-965653-32-6
Hardcover ISBN: 978-1-965653-33-3
Digital ISBN: 978-1-965653-34-0

www.GameChangerPublishing.com

DEDICATION

*For my three incredible daughters: Jessica, Tia, and Mikia.
Each of you fuels my desire to lead with integrity,
courage, and unwavering ambition.
My love for you goes beyond words.
Everything I have achieved reflects that.*

Read This First

Just to say thanks for buying and reading my book, I would like to give you a few free bonus gifts, no strings attached!

Scan the QR Code Here:

Neuro-Mastery

Unlocking Your Brain's Potential for Lasting Success

Dr. Pamela Seraphine

www.GameChangerPublishing.com

Foreword

If there's one thing we can be sure of on our journey of personal development and self-mastery, it's that our brain can be both our greatest asset and a most inexplicable adversary. Those of us who have worked in the field of psychotherapy for any length of time will attest to the enormous power of the brain to elevate us to great heights and reciprocally bring us down to the lowest depths. Often clients will be looking for answers "out there" when, in fact, the answers are within. That's not a cliche; it's a psycho-neurobiological fact. But how are we to navigate the seemingly complicated world of neurobiology to take hold of the keys to transformative change?

Fortunately, my colleague Dr. Pamela Seraphine has done the heavy lifting when it comes to turning the often complex field of neuroscience into a practical guide for everyday people wanting to awaken their untapped potential. What I appreciate about this book is that Dr. Seraphine has avoided the too-common empty platitudes and quick fixes and rather offers a comprehensive and scientifically-based roadmap to achieve true mastery over our lives by leveraging the positive power of our brains and avoiding the negatives. Following the advice in this book will most certainly rewrite the stories in your mind and soul that have been holding you back!

Dr. Seraphine has a unique blend of lived experience and scientific rigor that she applies in this book, providing practical and compassionate guidance. As a neuroscientist specializing in high performance and trauma recovery, she has a firm grasp on how the brain can both propel us toward greatness or sabotage our efforts. Her life is testimony of the human spirit's resiliency and the transforming potential of applied neuroscience. You are in good hands, knowing she has traveled the difficult path of gaining mastery over mind, body, and soul and can not only understand the path from a scientific perspective, but translate that understanding into this very practical book.

Dr. Seraphine guides us through a step-by-step process that challenges outdated narratives about mental toughness, willpower, and success, as she explains the inner workings of the brain. I appreciate how she explores trauma, chronic stress, and negative thought patterns and their potential to sabotage our goals and erode our sense of fulfillment, and then goes on to give us proven strategies leveraging neuroplasticity, emotional regulation, and soul integration for lasting change.

Bridging the gap between neuroscience, the wisdom of the soul, and practical intervention is not easy and requires a deep knowledge of the human condition and a talent to translate that into a pragmatic program. Dr. Seraphine does this remarkably well, expertly weaving together top-down and bottom-up approaches, providing a holistic framework that addresses the important facets of the human condition.

As readers, we are invited to question our long-held beliefs, release old patterns, and step into a new level of self-awareness. Through techniques like the G.L.A.D. Sleep Technique, the R.E.S.T., and Write-to-Right methods, Dr. Seraphine offers practical tools that are simple yet totally transformative. Her techniques demonstrate that our brain, when directed with intention and purpose, is our most powerful ally when it comes to living a life of authenticity, passion, and fulfillment.

I imagine that this book will become a lifeline for many who have felt trapped by their own thoughts, emotions, or circumstances. You could see this as a manifesto for anyone ready to break free from the limitations of the past and to step into a future of their own making.

It doesn't matter where you are in life. You may feel completely defeated and at a loss as to what to do next. This book will give you both hope and practical tools. You might be an accomplished individual looking to reach the next level in your career, a leader navigating the pressures of business and life, or simply someone seeking to live a more authentic and fulfilled life. Either way, this book will give you the tools, insights, and inspiration you need to master your mind and reclaim your destiny.

Matthew Dahlitz
Founder & CEO, *The Science of Psychotherapy*

Table of Contents

Introduction 1

Chapter 1 – The Truth About Your Brain 9

Chapter 2 – Regaining Conscious Control 25

Chapter 3 – Building a Formidable Soul 39

Chapter 4 – Conquering Inner Chaos 55

Chapter 5 – Creating Your Future Identity 71

Chapter 6 – Bulletproofing Your Values 85

Chapter 7 – Slaying Your Goals 97

Chapter 8 – Becoming the B.O.S.S. 115

Chapter 9 – Dominating Your Results Tracker 125

Chapter 10 – Firing on All Cylinders 137

Acknowledgments 143

About the Author 145

Endnotes 149

Introduction

Here's an uncomfortable truth: Your brain has the capacity to destroy your life without your conscious awareness. You won't even know it's happening. It can make you believe things that aren't true, remember things that never happened, push you to do things you shouldn't do, say things you shouldn't say, love people who aren't good for you, and hurt those you care about most. On top of that, it can sabotage your goals and block your path to lasting fulfillment. I can assure you: It's not fear that kills hope and dreams. It's not fear holding you back from what you know you're capable of. It's your brain. That's how powerful it is.

This isn't a small problem; *it's a huge f*cking problem.*

Here's another uncomfortable truth: Mental toughness and willpower alone aren't enough to achieve something great while maintaining your well-being. That's because no matter how mentally strong you are, you're still at the mercy of the inner workings of your brain. This isn't to say mental toughness isn't valuable—it absolutely is. Achieving your goals and creating the life you want would be nearly impossible without it.

But what I'm sharing with you in this book goes beyond mental toughness. If you're serious about goal achievement and lasting fulfillment, you must learn how to master your brain. If you don't, your brain will royally mess with your life.

Now, this might challenge your current beliefs, especially if you pride yourself on being mentally strong—or even being a badass mother**cker. You might even buy into the idea that stoicism holds the answers to all life's problems and challenges. But that's only part of the equation. Achieving your goals and maintaining a high-quality life takes much more than sheer mental strength.

Here's something you might not realize: Those people who seem to have it all together—the ones you admire the most—are probably suffering behind closed doors. This is a hidden problem buried beneath layers of bullsh*t and societal expectations. Our culture has made it clear: Leaders and high achievers, especially men, can never show weakness. Displaying anything less than elite strength, fortitude, courage, and fearlessness is practically forbidden.

If you're chasing greatness, this is the societal norm. But that doesn't make it right—or effective.

To make matters worse, psychology—the study of the mind—has dominated personal development and mental health services for the last century. The "mind" narrative has value, especially in times when neuroscience wasn't yet developed. But as powerful as it has been, it's not the whole story. It was only in the late 20th century, with the invention of neuroimaging and other technological advancements, that we developed the ability to actually see what happens in the brain when it's operating. It's only been just the last two decades that we've begun to fully understand the biological and chemical processes in the brain and nervous system and how they influence behavior and cognition.

Yet influential approaches to personal development, goal achievement, and trauma recovery remain deeply rooted in the mind narrative. This is largely because that narrative has been around the longest, with the most exposure and research backing it. But that doesn't necessarily make it the most effective or efficient approach for transforming your life and achieving what's most important to you.

Sure, you can try using that approach. But chances are you'll still experience significant psychological pain and emotional suffering along the way. And even if you do not recognize that it's happening to you, you'll end up inflicting it on others—because your brain is running the show, and that's a recipe for disaster. In all my experience, I've never met anyone who can intuitively distinguish between the workings of their brain, mind, body, or soul. But I'm going to show you how to do just that—though probably not in the way you're expecting.

First, let me give you some backstory so you can understand where I'm coming from.

From Misery to Mastery

I know this not just as a neuroscientist specializing in high performance and trauma recovery but also from deeply personal experience. I work primarily with highly successful men and women, and I can tell you that no matter how much status, wealth, or influence they've amassed, many of them are still suffering. It's a massive hidden problem within our society.

On the surface, they seem to have it all: they're in great shape, financially secure, and established in their careers. Yet, behind the scenes, their lives are falling apart. But you rarely hear about it—it's buried beneath layers of secrecy. They're dealing with lawsuits, relationship issues, divorces, addictions, depression, PTSD, sleep disturbances, and a host of medical problems.

I've lived through these challenges. I also developed the **Hope After Trauma Academy,** an online platform offering brain-based, trauma-informed education for individuals and organizations in high-stress industries. So, I've seen the transformative power of this knowledge firsthand, over and over again. My work is dedicated to helping people in these exact situations, guiding them from misery to mastery.

You can't outrun your brain. If you don't master it, it will dominate your life, and you will suffer. If you saw what I've seen behind the curtain, you'd have a completely different perspective on how far the mindset narrative alone can really take you.

I also know this struggle firsthand. There was a time when I believed that sheer willpower and relentless work ethic could overcome a lifetime of trauma, poverty, violence, victimization, and mental health challenges. I was determined to transform my life and achieve my dreams because I saw myself as the ultimate role model for my three daughters. They were my responsibility, and I knew I was already mentally tough—I'd survived more than most people could imagine.

But then life beat the hell out of me.

In 2008, my life took a devastating turn. I'd been a drummer since I was 12 years old, and after decades of chasing my dream of becoming a world-class percussionist, I suffered a career-ending shoulder injury that shattered everything I'd worked for. To make things worse, I was in the midst of a brutal divorce, with a vindictive ex seeking revenge. All I had were my three daughters—no support, no resources, no money, and no education.

I hit rock bottom, reaching a point at which I began meticulously planning to end my life.

The pain was unbearable, and I couldn't see any way out.

But then, unexpectedly, I found a glimmer of hope.

I enrolled in my first psychology course at university, taught by a neuroscientist. Those classes changed everything. The professor emphasized two key points that stuck with me. First, he said to never be afraid to challenge the status quo—that's what science is all about. Second, he talked at length about the brain's ability to completely hijack a person's thoughts, behaviors, and even their will to live.

He explained how the brain could drive someone to end their life without their conscious awareness. I didn't fully grasp the concept at the time, but it was enough to make me stop and consider that maybe—just maybe—my brain was at the root of my suffering.

As time went on, my life actually got worse. By 2010, I was still pushing myself far beyond my limits, and my circumstances remained extreme. I spiraled into a psychotic state. I began hearing voices, which was even more terrifying because of my family's history of schizophrenia. But when I first heard those voices, I remembered what my professor said, and something clicked: maybe this was my brain, not my soul. My soul didn't want to die. That realization was a turning point—it pulled me back from the edge.

Here's why that moment matters: Your brain is separate from your mind, body, and soul. At that breaking point, I realized something life-changing—my brain was reacting to the extreme stress I was under, but my soul, my true essence, was still intact. This distinction is vital for understanding how to take control of your life. I'll dive deeper into this throughout the book, but even if you don't read another word, remember this: Your brain is its own entity, separate from your mind, body, and soul.

I'm still incredibly grateful for the moment I was first introduced to neuroscience because something lit up inside me. It gave me a sense of purpose and set me on an unexpected new life mission. Had I not learned to master my brain and apply the principles of neuroscience, I wouldn't be here today sharing this with you. The insights and strategies I offer in this book are unique because they're born from both professional expertise and lived experience. My lifelong passion for drumming, coupled with my insatiable thirst for neuroscience, has shaped my work into something profoundly different from what you might expect—and that's a good thing.

The Neuro-Mastery methodologies I'll share with you saved my life. I live by these principles, and I teach them because they work. That's why I'm so passionate about passing this knowledge on to you. I hope the tools and insights you find in this book will be as transformative for you as they have been for me. Your quality of life is worth fighting for. Never forget that.

What is Neuro-Mastery?

Neuro-Mastery is the ability to harness your brain's full capacity to achieve personal excellence, lasting success, and deep fulfillment. It's a holistic approach that leverages the principles of applied neuroscience to optimize brain performance, transform your life, and help you achieve the goals that truly matter to you. Mastering your brain means learning how to get it to work for you, enabling sustainable and positive change.

Defining Personal Greatness

Personal greatness is the active pursuit of excellence and fulfillment through conscious, intentional choices. It's about aligning your actions with your core values and long-term goals, ensuring every decision supports your personal and professional growth. Achieving lasting success isn't just about external results—it's about cultivating a life that reflects what truly matters to you while maintaining well-being. What you consider truly great is unique to you—and that's exactly how it should be. It has to matter to you.

For me, it was going from being a high school dropout to earning my bachelor's degree in psychology, a master's of science in sports psychology, and eventually a doctorate in psychology with an emphasis in neuropsychology and neurobiology—earning all these degrees with honors. Those goals seemed impossible at one point—the odds were 100 percent against me, yet I achieved them. And that's what I consider pretty *f*cking great*. Nobody can take that away from me.

More importantly, the person I became in the process of reaching those goals is what truly matters. You have that same potential inside you. You might just be missing the skills to command your brain to do what you want—and that's exactly why I wrote this book for you.

Who Is This Book For?

This book isn't for everyone. It's not for those who resist self-awareness or don't value personal excellence. And it's definitely not for you if you're uncomfortable with raw, direct honesty. If you're determined to hold onto a victim mentality or the status quo, my teachings and my profanity will probably trigger you.

If you're ambitious and working toward excellence and success in your personal or professional life, this book is for you. If you've made mistakes, hurt others, done things you regret, or faced pain, fear, and setbacks on your path to growth, this book is also for you. If you're ready to acknowledge that what you've tried so far hasn't worked and are open to exploring new possibilities, you've got the right book in your hands.

This book will guide you toward lasting success and mastery, no matter your background. It's particularly valuable for those who work in high-stress environments—whether in business, healthcare, the military, first responders, entrepreneurship, athletics, the creative arts, or any field where managing stress, enhancing performance, and achieving long-term fulfillment are essential.

What This Book Offers

I wrote *Neuro-Mastery: Unlocking Your Brain's Potential for Lasting Success* as a step-by-step guide to help you master your brain and get it working to your advantage so you can transform your life for the better. This book offers actionable strategies to regain control of your life, optimize brain performance, and achieve the goals that truly matter to you. Be prepared to use unconventional brain-based methods to retrain your brain and learn how to overcome the challenges that have been sabotaging your progress.

This book also dives into addressing unresolved trauma and chronic stress, providing insights and strategies for healing and recovery. You'll learn about the importance of using top-down and bottom-up strategies, music as medicine, and how applied rhythmic entrainment can drive emotional recovery while building a resilient, integrated brain.

Neuro-Mastery also includes a 90-Day Sprint Goal Framework offering a practical approach to achieving your goals in the fastest time possible while maintaining your overall well-being. Through a detailed framework for personal excellence, this book will guide you toward aligning your actions with your core values, fostering holistic growth and fulfillment.

After reading this book, I hope you'll never let your brain destroy your life or drag you down the path of misery. I hope my words inspire you to actively pursue lasting success and live the life you want and deserve.

CHAPTER 1

The Truth About Your Brain

"When you judge another, you do not define them; you define yourself."
—Wayne Dyer

In this first chapter, I'm going to highlight four key facts about your brain and why it's vital for you to understand them. I've simplified these concepts so your brain doesn't reject them while you're reading. You'll soon learn why it does so. Yes, these topics are complex, but I'm breaking them down so you can apply them immediately. That's what matters: getting results.

Remember, no two brains are exactly alike. Your brain is radically different from anyone else's, yet the principles of applied neuroscience still apply to anyone with a brain. It's important to grasp how your brain operates and how it's influencing your life. Like I said earlier, your brain has the power to absolutely destroy your life if you let it—and that's a huge problem.

So, let's address it head-on.

Most of us have been taught to think of the brain as a supercomputer—brilliant, creative, and objective. But I see it more like today's advanced AI programs. Yes, it's incredibly intelligent, but like advanced AI, it can malfunction, give you the wrong information, or even lead to harmful outcomes. The truth is, we don't fully understand what the human brain is capable of—and that's both fascinating and unsettling.

What we do know is that we can use the science we have to transform your life—possibly even save it. It's about learning how to command your brain, influence its functioning, and optimize it so you can achieve greater success while maintaining your well-being and achieving fulfillment. It's not a choice between them—you can have it all.

The truth about your brain is that it's not an unchangeable entity. It's adaptable and capable of profound transformation. These four key facts will help you recognize your potential.

Fact #1: Your Brain Is the Primary Source of All Suffering

Your brain processes everything—emotions, feelings, perceptions, experiences, personality, and worldview. And all of that can be changed and improved. But you have to want to evolve. It requires conscious, intentional effort. Like I've said before, if you don't know how to master your brain, it will ruin your life without you even knowing it. You'll just think, *That's how life is,* or *That's just human nature.* But it's not.

We didn't have access to applied neuroscience principles in the past, but now we do. And while it's still early days in the field, we're making rapid progress.[1] What we do know is that every problem you face is processed through your brain. Your brain can make you do things without your conscious awareness while convincing you that you're in control. You'll think it's you making those decisions—but that's not necessarily true.

Chronic stress and trauma can change your brain's structure, chemistry, and functioning, whether you're aware of it or not.[2] That's a fact.

You don't get to choose how your brain responds to trauma or intense life experiences. It's not about what you think; it's about how your brain perceives it. Ignoring that is like having a mangled leg from a car accident and insisting it's fine. It's not fine—sometimes, you need someone to point out the obvious so that you're not delusional about your situation. The same goes for your brain. Chronic stress, trauma, and even positive experiences change your brain, and understanding this gives you control.

I know it's a bit confusing because the scientific narrative has muddled the message about the brain and mind. Trust me, I've been there. Even as a professional in this field, I had to wade through the confusion to figure it out. That's why I'm simplifying it for you now—so you can take practical steps to regain control and achieve your goals without letting your brain sabotage you. Throughout this book, I'm going to be dismantling many misconceptions.

One common misconception involves trauma's impact on the brain. You might think your past traumatic experiences didn't affect you. Maybe you've found yourself thinking, *It wasn't that serious,* or *It wasn't as bad as what others go through.* Maybe you compare your experience to that of military veterans or others and think, *Is it really the same?*

Yes, it is.

Take suicide as a powerful example. Your brain can be so persuasive that it might convince you to end your life as a form of protection. But the fact is suicidal thoughts, that inner voice, those relentless mental images—they all originate from your brain. You might think that voice is you, but it isn't. It's your brain's distorted logic, interpreting suicide as the ultimate solution to alleviate suffering. It's as if your brain is saying, "Life is too painful, so the only way to survive is to escape it altogether."

And yet, the popular narrative often frames it as "they didn't want to live" or blames the person, but that's simply not true. It's their brain, and they might not have had any control left. It's self-righteous to think *That could never happen to me.* If you have a brain, you're at risk. So are the people you care about. You don't know how their brains are functioning, and you might not recognize when their brains are malfunctioning. To fully grasp this premise, you must clearly distinguish the differences between your brain, mind, body, and soul. I'm getting to that.

We see a tragic example of this is the high suicide rates among first responders and military personnel.[4] Let me remind you, those are tough motherf*ckers. This isn't about mental weakness or lack of willpower—it's about brain health. Anyone with a brain can be struck down with brain health issues. Globally, more than 700,000 people die by suicide every year, making it one of the leading causes of death worldwide.[5] Suicidal thoughts are often a sign that the brain is misfiring. It's not a weakness, but it's hidden because everyone feels the need to act tough. But it's happening whether we talk about it or not.

Any brain can misfire and cause deep misery, but it can also be recalibrated to bring happiness, joy, vitality, and passion.

I know this because I've lived it. This isn't just about academic knowledge or achievements—this is deep, lived experience. I know what it's like for your brain to take over, driving you into a psychotic state and making you want to end your life. If I hadn't applied these principles, I wouldn't be alive today to share this with you. I'll say it again, I'm passionate about this because I know the truth: Mental toughness and willpower alone aren't enough. They're part of the equation, but you're missing the other half if you don't learn how to master your brain. I'm not here just to tell you the bad stuff. The good news is coming, I promise.

Fact #2: Your Brain Is Your Protector

Your brain is wired to protect your survival at all costs, not push you toward growth and progress. But again, your brain can misfire. It can feed you the wrong information, keeping you in a constant state of perceived threat, even when it doesn't make any logical sense—and you won't even realize it's happening.[6]

Let's consider the COVID pandemic. We reached a point where even the air we breathed and other human beings became threats to our survival. The structure and functioning of our brains were altered, and now we're grappling with collective trauma. Collective trauma refers to the psychological and emotional impact experienced by a group or community because of a shared event—or series of events—that causes widespread distress, disruption, and upheaval. This trauma extends beyond individual experiences and affects entire populations, often resulting in deep-seated feelings of fear, helplessness, and grief.

The snowball effect is real, and it's only beginning to show up in high achievers and ambitious leaders—maybe even you. There is a good chance the strategies that once worked for you might not be working anymore. That's because your brain has changed.

Your brain is constantly scanning for threats—real or perceived—even if nothing's happening. The most counter-intuitive part is that this threat response includes anything that might bring you closer to happiness, joy, or fulfillment. This means your brain will sabotage you, especially if you haven't experienced those positive emotions in a long time. If you've lost your way, if you're suffering behind closed doors where no one can see, I get it. I see it all the time with my clients. Even when they start feeling better and making progress, I know their brain is about to sabotage them.

When you read this book and start applying the strategies, and they start working, get ready for your brain to kick in with *This isn't worth it. This won't work. What's she talking about?* Your brain will try to shut you down. You need to be aware of that.

I always warn my clients: Watch out for happiness and positive emotions. Your brain will resist them, and you'll buy into the lie that if you really wanted it badly enough, you'd achieve your goals and have the life you want.

Don't fall for that. It doesn't work like that.

When you can't reach your goals or climb out of living six feet under like I did, you end up blaming yourself. *What's wrong with me? Everyone else is mentally tough and successful. They've mastered their life—why can't I?*

I'll tell you why.

You've got a completely different brain. That's why. You need to figure out what will work for your brain—what will make your brain work to your advantage. That's what this is about. And yes, it's possible.

Fact #3: Your Brain Is a Physical Entity

Your brain is a powerful physical entity that operates through complex neural networks driven by neurochemical and biochemical processes.[7] It's constantly changing and adapting, and you have the opportunity to influence what thrives and what fades away.

Here's the truth:

You are not your brain. You are your soul.

Let me explain.

Your physical brain is an extraordinary processor responsible for the automatic, subconscious functions that govern much of your daily life—behaviors, reactions, and bodily functions that operate seamlessly without your direct input. Yet, these processes are not fixed; they can be reshaped and guided through intentional mastery.

Your mind, a metaphysical interpreter, works in tandem with your brain to process, analyze, and give meaning to your thoughts, emotions, and experiences. Your body, however, is not just a passive vessel—it's a powerful and dynamic force that acts as the interface between your mind and the physical world. Through your body, you carry out actions, regulate your energy, and embody the changes your brain and mind work to achieve.

But your soul? The soul is the essence of your conscious awareness—your deepest self, beyond the mind and body. It is your life force, the source of your true identity, guiding your sense of purpose and enabling you to make intentional, meaningful choices that align with your highest potential.

Together, the brain, mind, and body form the interconnected framework through which you navigate and experience the world. Yet it is your soul that directs the conscious, purposeful aspect of who you are. If the term "soul" doesn't resonate with you, call it your conscious self, authentic self, true self, higher self, spirit, or even your God-like self—whatever reflects the essence of who you are. What matters is recognizing that this essence isn't just a product of your brain's automatic processes. It is something far greater.

To be clear, I'm not here to challenge any religious or spiritual beliefs you may hold. When I speak of the "soul," I'm referring to your conscious self—your core essence. That's what truly matters in this context.

Here's the main point: To truly transform your life and create lasting, sustainable change, you must separate your brain from your soul. That's the only way to conquer the inner workings of your brain and get it to work for you, instead of against you.

From a neuroscientific perspective, you need to use your mind and body to retrain your brain. When you utilize thoughts and images to retrain your brain—that's your mind at work. When you use your physiology to retrain your brain—that's the body at work. But without a doubt, you must use your soul to command your mind and body to retrain your brain. That's the key to achieving lasting success and fulfillment. You need to build what I call a formidable soul—a strong soul that can command your brain to do what your soul desires.

Many of my clients—high achievers who struggle behind closed doors—come to me completely disconnected from the idea of having a soul. They've spent years relying solely on sheer willpower to climb the ladder of success. Willpower is your brain's conscious effort to push you through challenges, and while it's powerful, it's also limited. The more you lean on willpower without addressing the deeper part of yourself—your soul—the more drained, frustrated, and unfulfilled you become.

Now, here's the problem: If you haven't addressed your soul, I guarantee it's slowly dying. You might not even realize it because your brain has convinced you that your problems, limitations, and lack of fulfillment are all caused by external factors—your job, other people, circumstances beyond your control. It's the classic "It's not me, it's them" mentality. But here's the truth:

Your brain is lying to you.

Your brain, operating on subconscious processes, can easily distract you with external pursuits and keep you focused on things that don't truly matter. And when you rely on willpower alone, you end up disconnecting from your soul—your true self. This creates a disconnect where you're so busy fighting external and internal battles that you lose touch with the very thing that brings you lasting fulfillment.

So, while willpower can get you far, it will never be enough on its own. You have to recognize that your soul is the true source of power that unlocks the potential of your brain. Only by aligning your soul with your brain, mind, and body can you create real, lasting change. If you continue to ignore your soul, you'll stay stuck in cycles of unfulfillment or burnout, and no amount of willpower will fix that.

It often feels like *I've worked so hard, so why do I feel so empty?* Or maybe you're stuck in the loop of, *I'm doing everything right, but nothing feels meaningful anymore.* Perhaps you've poured yourself into your career, your family, or a cause you care about, but now you're exhausted, burned out, and questioning what it was all for. You might even be wondering, *Is this really all there is?*

Or, you're on the other end—hustling, grinding, chasing your dreams—yet no matter how hard you push, you still feel stuck, unable to break through to where you want to be. That's your brain in control.

It's confusing as hell because you've probably been thinking that your mindset or life itself is the problem. It's not. The real issue is that your soul is dying, and your brain is dominating your life.

That's why, when I work with a client on the brink of giving up—so close to ending it all—I immediately know that their soul is dying. They haven't nurtured, fed, or strengthened it. They might not even know it exists because they've been too busy trying to be mentally tough and force their way through life, wondering why they've lost their passion and will to live.

Even if you don't think this applies to you, keep reading. I guarantee your future self is going to need to embody this premise. I'm going to show you exactly how to rebuild and strengthen your soul, step by step. Call it whatever you want, but I'm calling it your soul because I know what it's like to have my soul almost completely die. I also know what it's like to sell my soul and have to earn it back. I don't want that to happen to you. This is hard-earned wisdom.

Fact #4: Your Brain Has the Ability to Change

Your brain's ability to change is known as neuroplasticity. That means you have the potential to retrain, rewire neural pathways, and enhance the structure and functioning of your brain through repetitive practice.[9] You have that spectacular ability. Self-directed neuroplasticity is the conscious, intentional effort to modify brain connections and neural pathways to respond in healthier ways to life's challenges. You can do that through the repetitive processes—brain-based strategies—that I'll be sharing with you throughout this book.

Self-directed neuroplasticity is your brain's powerful tool for unlocking lasting success and fulfillment. But even with that, if you focus solely on your brain and ignore what your soul truly desires, you'll end up repeating the same cycles. I'll say it again—if you want to achieve your goals quickly and sustainably, you have to master your brain by aligning it with your soul's deepest intentions.

Your soul must command your brain, mind, and body to work in harmony toward your personal greatness.

You must embody that intention. You must define success and fulfillment on your own terms. It's essential to know exactly what a meaningful, fulfilled life looks like for you. It doesn't matter how others define success—this is your life, and you're responsible for creating it. And yes, that's going to require massive action and a formidable soul.

From a neuroscientific perspective, it takes approximately 67 days of consistent practice to modify neural networks, rewire them, and enhance them.[10] Your habits, thoughts, beliefs, identity, and even your worldview can all be changed through self-directed neuroplasticity.

It's simple. But it's not easy.

That's why I'm giving you the 90-Day Sprint Goal Framework to make this possible for you. And no, it has nothing to do with athleticism. It's an effective way to achieve your goals in the fastest time frame possible by using the premise of 90 days to retrain your brain. I'll dive into the details later in the book.

Your brain and soul need this structure—a system in place. You've got to give yourself 90 days at a time to transform, evolve, and create tangible results. Earlier, I mentioned 67 days, but it actually takes time to figure out what you want fully. I always suggest you structure retraining your brain in 90-day increments. You need short timeframes and consistent efforts to create lasting positive change. After that, the process goes on repeat indefinitely. If you've done it right, you'll never want to be without this 90-day framework. The results will speak for themselves—and they'll be screaming, "Repeat, repeat, repeat!"

*****

Let's take a moment to clarify a few key points.

There are three primary ways to change your brain: using your mind, using your body, and using external sources. Medication is one external source, and yes, you might need it to keep your brain in check. I'm not against medication if it serves a viable purpose. But even if you're on meds, you still need to learn how to master your brain and get it working for you. Otherwise, the same issues will keep following you throughout your life.

Other external options, like biofeedback, electrostimulation, and various therapies, may or may not be necessary for you. But no matter what, you must use top-down strategies (addressing changes in the higher cortical areas of your brain) and bottom-up, body-based strategies (addressing the lower and mid-level areas of the brain). And once again, it's your soul that drives this transformation.

As I mentioned, the common narrative focuses on using the mind to change the brain. But you can't ignore the role of your body and soul. You can't pretend the mind alone is the holy grail—it just doesn't work that way. If you're experiencing suffering, burnout, cynicism, overwhelm, pain, anger, or frustration, it's likely because your approach is incomplete. To achieve personal excellence, success, and lasting fulfillment, you need to engage all parts of yourself—you need to be firing on all cylinders.

You don't need to be more resilient. You need to build a resilient, integrated brain.

That's the goal.

That's what's going to change your life.

That's huge.

It doesn't matter whether you're chasing greatness or pursuing smaller goals. No matter what your target is, you need these strategies in place so your brain doesn't sabotage your ability to achieve what matters most to you.

That's all that matters. You absolutely have that capability. And, of course, self-awareness is the starting point of any transformational change.

Why My Work Is a New Approach, Not a Repackaging of Old Concepts

You might be thinking, *The concept of the soul isn't exactly new, right? People have been discussing the mind and the soul for centuries. So how is this any different?* And I get it—on the surface, it might seem like I'm just revisiting concepts that have been around for a long time.

But let me explain why this approach is something entirely different.

While the soul has long been a topic of discussion, modern neuroscience gives us a deeper understanding of the brain and how it can be reshaped. What sets my work apart is the integration of cutting-edge brain science with the timeless wisdom of the soul. It's about mastering both your brain *and* your soul to achieve real, transformative growth.

We now know that through neuroplasticity, you have the power to rewire your brain and change your life. But here's the thing: If you focus only on your brain, you'll miss the deeper potential your soul holds. My work is about aligning and creating synergy between the mind, body, brain, and soul that allows you to unlock your full potential.

This isn't just about thinking differently—it's about living differently.

It's not enough to navigate the subconscious mind or rely on willpower alone. You need a holistic system that connects the dots between brain science and the deeper truths about who you are at your core. That's the evolution of Neuro-Mastery that's possible today. It's a practical, actionable system that merges scientific insights with soul-level transformation.

That's what makes this work new, revolutionary, and powerful. It's not just about understanding your mind; it's about mastering your brain and your soul together to create lasting change in your life.

The Five Levels of Learning Competency

Before you move forward with the next chapter, I want to ask you where you see yourself on the five levels of learning competency. Typically, there are four levels, but I've added a fifth because, over the years, I've identified a critical level that is rarely discussed.

Level 1: Unconsciously Incompetent

You're unaware of the skills or knowledge that you lack. This is where most people find themselves. This was definitely me when I first stumbled into the field of neuroscience. Back then, it never even crossed my mind that my brain shouldn't be in charge—and that I could learn to master it.

Level 2: Consciously Incompetent

You're now aware of how little you know and recognize the need to learn more. If you picked up this book, chances are you're already here and aware that you're missing key knowledge and skills. That's a great place to be—it means you're ready to learn.

Level 3: Consciously Competent

You've developed a solid understanding and have become skilled in using your brain to work in your favor. You can consciously apply what you've learned and are looking to take your abilities to the next level. Maybe that's where you're at right now.

Level 4: Unconsciously Competent

At this stage, your skills have become second nature. You apply them effortlessly and almost without thinking. You're no longer just trying—you're living it. Trust me, you still need to continue reading this book.

Level 5: Meta-Unconsciously Competent

This is the level where you've moved beyond being unconsciously competent and may believe that anyone can change if they just want it bad enough. But here's the harsh truth—this level can be dangerous.

Not everyone has the same capacity for change. The reality is that some people have sustained significant brain injuries or have notable differences in brain structure and neural functioning, which might limit their ability to change. It's not that there's no hope, but the idea that anyone can change just by wanting it is overly simplistic and, frankly, unrealistic.

Everyone's circumstances are different, and each brain is entirely unique. My goal with this book is to give you a chance to see if you have the capacity to master your brain to achieve personal excellence, success, and lasting fulfillment.

For the record, my level of competency fluctuates between levels 3 and 4. I've mastered everything I teach. However, there are still an unlimited number of subjects where I'm unconsciously incompetent and unaware of what they are.

Mastering your brain isn't a one-time achievement; it's a lifelong journey of self-mastery, empowerment, and sustainable positive change. As you progress through this book, you'll gain the tools and strategies needed to take command of your brain, but remember—this is a continuous process. The pursuit of mastery isn't about perfection; it's about consistent growth and intentional action. My hope is that you'll take the strategies I share, apply them to your life, and strive for mastery in your own unique way.

Chapter 1 Takeaways

Don'ts:

- **Don't assume your brain is working in your best interest.** Your brain is primarily designed for survival, not fulfillment or growth. Left unchecked, it can sabotage your goals and your quality of life.
- **Don't believe that mental toughness alone is enough.** Relying solely on willpower while ignoring how your brain works will lead to burnout, frustration, and limited progress.
- **Don't overlook the connection between your brain, mind, body, and soul.** Ignoring one part of the equation—especially your soul—leaves you incomplete and vulnerable to self-sabotage.
- **Don't underestimate the power of your brain.** Your brain can convince you that external factors are the problem when the real issue may lie within your own neural patterns.

Do's:

- **Do see your brain as a separate entity from your mind, body, and soul.** Understanding this distinction is critical for mastering your brain and achieving sustainable change.
- **Do embrace self-directed neuroplasticity.** You have the power to retrain your brain through conscious effort, repetitive practice, and intentional strategies.
- **Do focus on building a strong, formidable soul.** Your soul is what drives your mind and body to retrain your brain. Strengthen it to command your brain effectively.
- **Do take a comprehensive approach to brain mastery.** Use top-down (mind) and bottom-up (body) strategies, and never forget that your soul is the linchpin that holds it all together.
- **Do embrace the 90-Day Sprint Goal Framework.** I'll explain this more in the upcoming chapters, but the premise is that using short, focused timeframes with consistent effort is key to retraining your brain and creating transformation.

Chapter 1 Summary: The Truth About Your Brain

You've just taken the first step to understanding the truth about your brain: how it can be both your greatest asset and your biggest obstacle. This chapter revealed that you're not just a mind or a body—you are a powerful soul capable of commanding your brain to work in your favor. You now know that mastery is about integrating all aspects of who you are and applying the principles of neuroscience to achieve greatness on your terms.

It doesn't matter where you're starting from or what challenges you've faced. You have the ability to change your brain, transform your life, and reach new levels of success and fulfillment. But it's going to require intentional action, self-awareness, and a relentless commitment to mastering the strategies that work for you.

As you move forward, remember this: True mastery is about more than just thinking your way through life. It's about aligning your mind, body, and soul to become the person you're meant to be. You have one life to live—own it, embrace it, and get ready to take command of your brain like never before.

Myth 1: Pushing through fatigue builds mental toughness.

Truth: Your brain actually performs worse when you constantly push through exhaustion. Science shows that rest and recovery are crucial for optimizing brain performance and cognitive function, especially if you want long-term success (Smith, 2011). Yes, you need to become mentally tough, but you must also consider your neurobiological limits.

CHAPTER 2

Regaining Conscious Control

"Discipline equals freedom. If you can't control yourself, you will be controlled."
–Jocko Willink

Let's break down what it really means to regain conscious control of your brain. I get it—it sounds complicated. But as I've mentioned (and will keep mentioning throughout this book), your brain can absolutely destroy your life if you let it. If you don't master it, it will control you. Whether you're aware of it or not, it's happening—because your brain is naturally wired to work against you.

You've got to learn how to take back control and command your brain to do what you want. The truth is, your brain is both brilliant and destructive. Without conscious control, it'll lead your life down a path of ruin (or, as I like to call it, the path of f*ckery). The problem most people face—and this might include you—is that they can't distinguish between the voice of their brain and the voice of their soul.

Give it a try: Can you honestly tell the difference between the voice that's coming from your brain and the one that's coming from your soul?

Even if you think you can, I'd challenge that belief. Don't believe everything you think.

There are plenty of books out there on the conscious and subconscious mind, yet I've never met anyone who fully understands the difference between their brain and their soul. Let alone hear them clearly.

But whether you can or not, you need to strengthen this capacity—to know without a doubt which voice is which—because your brain will sound a lot like your soul. That's where the excuses come from. That's why you do stupid things, make terrible choices, and sabotage your own life.

You'll look back and think, *Why did I do that?*

Well, I know why. Your brain likes to sound like the logical conductor of your life.

Why didn't you follow through on what you know you should do?

Because your brain was running the show.

Why do you keep repeating the same mistakes?

Because your brain is running the show.

It's controlling everything.

In other words, that voice in your head and those thoughts you're hearing—most of the time (about 95% of the time)—are subconscious programming. It's previous conditioning of neural pathways, reinforced by neurochemistry, biochemistry, and other factors.[1] But here's the point once again: That's not who you are. That's not your soul, your conscious self. That's your brain.

Untangling Your Inner Dialogue

You must always be aware that your brain can often mimic the voice of your soul—your conscious self. The internal dialogue in your head might feel like a conversation between your brain and your soul, but most of the time, it's just your brain rationalizing with itself, using past experiences and subconscious programming. The key is learning to distinguish between the two. Until you can hear the difference between your brain's automatic thoughts and your soul's true voice, it's easy to confuse the two.

For example, after setting a goal, you might catch yourself saying, *I don't feel like doing it. I've got other things to do, and it doesn't really matter.* That's your brain talking 100 percent.

It gets even more confusing because the popular narrative is that if someone makes a choice, they are in control.

We hear things like, "They chose to do something terrible," "They chose not to turn their life around," "They chose to give up," or even "They chose not to change for the better."

But it's not that simple.

That's why I'm saying if you believe that anyone can just choose differently if they want it bad enough, you're missing the bigger picture. Not everyone has full control of their brain. Some people have impaired brain function or diminished capacity in areas that directly affect decision-making.[2] Every brain is different.

We have no right to judge someone else's choices without understanding how their brain is actually functioning.

This is about bringing some compassion and empathy back to humanity. We need to stop pretending we know how someone else's brain is operating. It's tough—I get that. It's hard to separate whether someone's actions are driven by conscious choice or by brain dysfunction.

I see this plenty, especially when it comes to partner betrayal. When someone cheats on their spouse, the betrayed partner might think, *They chose to do that,* or *They knew how much it would hurt me, but they did it anyway.* And the one who betrayed their partner often says, "I don't know why I did it. I just did."

It's complicated.

*****

In a perfect world, people would always keep the promises they make—to themselves and to others. But they don't. The only thing we can be sure of is that their brain processed the decision. Now, they might appear to be acting consciously, fully aware of their actions, but the reality is far more complex. Was their prefrontal cortex—the part of the brain responsible for rational thinking and impulse control—fully engaged? Do they have the capacity for self-regulation and higher-order thinking? Or were they operating from the more primitive, survival-driven parts of the brain? We don't know.[3]

But here's the truth: even if they were acting from those lower levels of consciousness, there are still consequences. Poor decisions, whether driven by subconscious impulses or external pressures, have a ripple effect. People still have to live with the aftermath of their choices.

I've seen clients struggle with this time and time again—believing they were making conscious choices, only to realize later that their decisions were driven by fear or unresolved patterns. When they finally stepped back and aligned with their soul's deeper wisdom, their entire outlook changed.

However, taking it personally, pointing fingers, or assigning blame for anything beyond your control is a waste of your energy. It doesn't fuel change; it fuels resentment. And that's a cycle that leads to nowhere but more self-induced suffering.

Conscious Evolution

What's the solution? Objectivity. You've got to step outside the emotional storm and understand that while consequences are inevitable, blame and shame are not necessarily a productive approach to change. If it doesn't lead to growth, healing, or transformation, then it's not productive. In fact, they only reinforce the very patterns you're trying to break free from.

I'm sharing this with you because you might believe that your decisions are aligned with your true self, but they could be completely out of sync with your soul's true desires. The brain is powerful, but it doesn't always operate in harmony with your soul. Your decisions, even when they seem rational or well-considered, could be driven by outdated patterns, impulses, or fears—none of which reflect who you really are or who you want to become.

Remember, this isn't about condemning yourself for past decisions. It's about recognizing that you're capable of so much more.

The next time you think *Why did I do that?*—become aware that your brain made that choice based on previous conditioning, experiences, neurochemistry, and existing neural pathways. Your brain is constantly picking up perceived threats, integrating ideas and stimuli, feeding your beliefs, and altering your perception of reality as if it's the absolute truth. Just because you perceive something a certain way doesn't make it true.

From a brain-based perspective, there are plenty of things that can go wrong. You could have diminished brain functioning or structural damage from childhood trauma, chronic stress, or other life challenges.[4]

As I said earlier, it doesn't matter whether you think your childhood was "that bad" or if emotional abuse, psychological abuse, workplace harassment, or chronic stress affected you. Your brain decides how it processes those experiences—not your conscious self. Remember, only about 5 percent of your conscious self (your soul) is actively involved in decision-making.

The good news? You can develop higher levels of consciousness. But remember, this is a continuous state of conscious evolution. You don't master your brain once and then coast through life—you never know what's coming down the pipeline.

Maybe you've had a great life so far. If so, you're one of the few and far between. Even then, you still need to master your brain and strengthen your soul because you don't know what challenges lie ahead. You don't know how your brain will interpret real or perceived threats when they arise. Sustainable fulfillment and success come from harmonizing a disciplined brain with an empowered soul, guiding you to achieve your highest potential. When you embody that premise, you'll tap into your divine potential.

*****

The G.L.A.D. Sleep Technique: Taking Command of Your Brain

Now, back to the original premise about discerning the difference between your brain and your soul. I promised you a technique that works, and I use it with every single client. It's called the G.L.A.D. Sleep Technique, originally created by Dr. Robert A. Emmons. I've adapted and refined it significantly to fit my approach, but the core principles remain the same, and just as effective.

The name might sound unrelated to taking conscious control, but trust me, it's directly connected. I'm going to walk you through each step, explain why it works, and show you how it's the perfect starting point for hearing the difference between your brain and your soul.

The G.L.A.D. Sleep technique is designed to create restorative sleep by taking control of your brain before bed, ensuring a restful night. If you're not taking control of your brain before sleep, you're letting it run wild. And when you let your brain do whatever it wants, it will absolutely mess with your sleep.

Many of my clients struggle with insomnia because they let their brains run the show at the end of the day.

> *Never let your brain do whatever it wants—that's a hard no.*

Keep in mind that overcoming insomnia isn't a one-size-fits-all solution; it's complex. However, this technique is a powerful tool to add to your Neuro-Mastery toolkit. Even if you don't have sleep disturbances, I encourage you to still try this technique. It's a bit of a weird process to start differentiating between your brain and your soul. This technique works well at bedtime because it's often the only time you have a solid chance of having no distractions. It's just your brain and your soul.

Heads up: Your brain will likely reject this technique, claiming it's too simple to work. That's to be expected. Push through and keep moving forward.

G.L.A.D. stands for Grateful, Learned, Achieved, and Danced. I know that might not make sense yet, but I'm going to break it down for you. This technique is a practical demonstration of how your thoughts and actions can reshape neural pathways. I want you to apply it in real-time. That means once I explain it, I want you to implement the G.L.A.D. technique for seven straight days—before you even finish reading this book. Why? Because I want you to experience the results of self-directed neuroplasticity and start to recognize the difference between your brain and your soul.

Here's what you do:

Right before bed—no distractions, no phones, no writing anything down—just you, your brain, and your soul. You must consciously and intentionally force your brain to answer these four questions:

1. What are three things I'm grateful for?
2. What are three things I learned today?
3. What are three things I achieved today?
4. What are three things that made my heart dance?

Now, you might be thinking this sounds too easy to be effective. Trust me—it's much harder than it seems. Here's what's likely to happen: First, your brain might say, "This is never going to work." Or maybe you'll try it for a day or two, and your brain will tell you it's a waste of time. Then your brain will bombard you with every excuse imaginable to stop you from continuing. You'll hear things like:

- I don't need to do this.
- I'm too tired.
- I don't even know what I'm grateful for.
- I didn't learn anything today.
- I didn't achieve anything today.

All that mental chatter? That's your brain. You've got to get your soul to command your brain to answer those damn questions every night. Don't give it a choice. Your soul must take full dominance.

Here's how this usually plays out:

1. What are three things I'm grateful for? This is often the easiest to answer.
2. What are three things I learned today? This one starts to challenge your brain.
3. What are three things I achieved today? By this point, your brain might get bored.
4. What are three things that made my heart dance? Now, your brain goes blank, convincing you nothing brought you joy, excitement, or happiness.

Once again, you must force your brain to answer these questions.

It might sound simple, but following through is tough. You've probably never considered that you could command your brain like this. You might think those excuses and lack of responses are you—they're not.

Every time you force your brain to do what you tell it to, that's your soul speaking to your brain.

That's your conscious self finally taking control. If you can't follow through, it means your brain is in charge, and you're living at its mercy.

The beginner level is seven days straight. Mastering conscious control using this sleep technique takes 90 days. After that, you'll have physically retrained your brain, and you will have formed a new valuable habit. The bonus is that you should be able to distinguish between your brain and your soul. Your soul forced your brain to do what you told it to do. Your soul would never bring you further away from what it is you want. This is extremely important to remember!

Why the G.L.A.D. Sleep Technique Helps You Discern Between the Voice of Your Brain and the Voice of Your Soul

One of the primary reasons the G.L.A.D. Sleep Technique is so effective at helping you differentiate between the voice of your brain and the voice of your soul lies in how it targets the brain's conscious and subconscious processing. Let's break down the brain-based reasoning behind why this technique works:

1. **Interrupting Automatic Thought Patterns:** As mentioned, the thoughts and beliefs you carry throughout the day are often on autopilot, influenced by previous conditioning and ingrained neural pathways. By intentionally practicing the G.L.A.D. Technique before sleep, you are disrupting these automatic loops and forcing your brain to engage in conscious reflection. This allows you to access deeper layers of awareness—where your soul, or conscious self, resides. Over time, you'll notice a distinct shift in how the responses come to you: Those driven by the brain tend to be reactive and fear-based, while those arising from your soul are more aligned with your values and authentic desires.

2. **Activating Different Brain Regions:** When you ask yourself what you're grateful for, what you've learned, what you've achieved, and what made your heart dance, you're engaging both the prefrontal cortex (responsible for higher-order thinking) and the limbic system (involved in emotion and memory).[5] The voice of your brain usually comes from a place of past conditioning and survival, driven by the more primitive parts of your brain. Meanwhile, the voice of your soul taps into the prefrontal cortex, where purpose, meaning, and long-term goals reside. As you consciously direct your brain to reflect on positive and growth-oriented experiences, you begin to separate reactive thought patterns from those that are more in tune with your deeper self.

3. **Strengthening the Connection Between Thought and Emotion:** The G.L.A.D. Technique bridges the gap between rational thought and emotional experience. When you ask what made your heart dance, you are diving into the realm of your soul—the part of you that seeks joy, fulfillment, and purpose. By regularly reflecting on these questions, you train your brain to make this connection more consistently. Over time, you'll be able to clearly sense the difference between thoughts that are brain-generated (often focused on fear, stress, and negativity) and those that stem from your soul (focused on alignment, purpose, and authentic joy).

4. **Building Metacognitive Awareness:** One of the most powerful benefits of the G.L.A.D. Technique is that it develops your metacognitive awareness: the ability to think about what you're thinking about. This practice is key to discerning the voice of your brain from the voice of your soul. When you consistently practice self-reflection, you begin to recognize patterns in your thoughts, beliefs, and emotions. You'll start to notice which thoughts are rooted in your brain's programming and which thoughts come from a place of deeper truth. This awareness is critical for taking conscious control of your brain and living in alignment with your soul's desires.

5. **Reinforcing Positive Neural Pathways While Quieting Negative Ones:** Always remember that the brain has a natural tendency to focus on the negative—it's wired for survival. By intentionally focusing on positive reflections before sleep, you're counteracting this tendency and building neural pathways that are more aligned with growth, gratitude, and fulfillment.[6] Over time, the patterns associated with stress, fear, and self-doubt weaken, while those associated with joy, learning, and purpose become stronger. The more these positive pathways are reinforced, the clearer it becomes which thoughts are brain-generated and which are soul-driven.

To recap: the G.L.A.D. Sleep Technique works because it directly engages the parts of your brain responsible for self-awareness, emotional regulation, and self-reflection. By consistently practicing this technique, you'll develop the ability to discern when your brain is steering you off course and when your soul is guiding you toward what it truly desires. And this is just the beginning!

It's a simple yet powerful tool that sets the foundation for regaining conscious control. Over time, you'll start to hear the difference when your soul commands your brain to align with your highest intentions and desires.

Chapter 2 Takeaways

Don'ts:

- **Don't mistake your brain's thoughts for your soul's voice.** Most of your thoughts are the product of unconscious programming, not your true self-speaking.
- **Don't take your thoughts at face value.** Just because something feels true doesn't mean it is. Your brain is designed to deceive you with thinking traps and flawed logic.
- **Don't assume you have full control over your decisions.** Impaired brain function, trauma, and conditioning can sabotage your choices without you even realizing it.
- **Don't rely on willpower alone.** Personal excellence and lasting fulfillment come from mastering the harmony between your brain, mind, body, and soul—not sheer determination.

Do's:

- **Do learn to discern between your brain and your soul.** Start developing the capacity to distinguish between the voices in your head and what your true self is guiding you toward.
- **Do challenge your thoughts, beliefs, and perceptions regularly.** Engage in metacognition to break free from autopilot and take conscious control.

- **Do adopt techniques like the G.L.A.D. Sleep Technique.** Use practical methods to retrain your brain, gain conscious control, and regain your personal power.
- **Do recognize that Neuro-Mastery is a continuous journey.** It isn't about quick fixes; it's about consistent, small actions that lead to profound, lasting change.

Chapter 2 Summary: Regaining Conscious Control

In this chapter, we dug into what it truly means to regain conscious control of your brain. The harsh truth is that most of your thoughts, beliefs, and behaviors are driven by unconscious programming. Without realizing it, you're likely on autopilot—letting your brain dictate your life's direction and sabotage your true desires.

Taking back control means learning to tell the difference between the voice of your brain and the voice of your soul. It's about challenging the lies your brain tells you and developing a higher level of consciousness that allows you to align your actions with your core values and purpose.

I also introduced the G.L.A.D. Sleep Technique—a straightforward yet powerful method to start retraining your brain at the end of each day. This technique will help you connect with your soul's desires and build a brain that works for you instead of against you.

Mastering your brain is challenging, but so is living a life filled with suffering, regret, and a compromised soul. You have two options: intentionally evolve, or risk your brain dragging you down into misery. Transformation doesn't happen overnight, but the journey is worth it. You can either command your brain to evolve or be held hostage by it. The decision is yours—choose wisely.

Myth 2: Left-brained and right-brained people are fundamentally different.

Truth: The idea that people are either "left-brained" or "right-brained" is outdated. Modern neuroscience shows that both hemispheres are involved in almost all cognitive tasks, and it's the communication between them that drives creativity and problem-solving (Nielsen et al., 2013). This is why I repeatedly state that for lasting success and fulfillment, you need to build an integrated, resilient brain. Higher levels of connectivity are key!

CHAPTER 3

Building a Formidable Soul

*"It's ok to be f*cked up. It's not ok to stay that way."*
–Sergeant John Kelly (ret.)

The essence of sustaining personal excellence requires a dual focus. On the one hand, you've got to optimize your brain functioning:

- Enhance your cognitive abilities.
- Take conscious control.
- Make your brain work for you (not against you).
- Improve focus, performance, and productivity.
- Maintain a lifestyle that supports brain health.

That's one side of the equation. The other side? Building a formidable soul—a strong, passionate, and invigorated inner self that commands your brain to follow your deepest desires.

Your soul is the core of who you really are, and that part of you deserves your commitment. Building a formidable soul means aligning your actions with your values, growing intentionally, and diving into the things that light you up—whether they make sense to others or not. Research highlights that living in alignment with your values builds resilience and fulfillment.[1] This includes embracing every part of yourself—the good, the bad, and the downright ugly. When you combine brain optimization with soul cultivation, you're not just sharp; you're unshakable, grounded in who you are, and ready to dominate every area of your life.

Cutting Through the Nonsense

A lot of people are stuck in feelings of chaos because society's messaging has lost touch with what it means to be fully human. Too many people get caught up in the nonsense of believing that "all feelings are valid"—and I'm here to tell you that's straight-up false. Neuroscientific research shows that not all thoughts or feelings are accurate, and that challenging maladaptive neural patterns is key for mental health and cognitive resilience.[2] We've got to challenge the lies we've been fed and get back to what's real. Not all thoughts or feelings are true or helpful.

Emotions vs. Feelings: The Distinction That Matters

This is a big topic, but allow me to give you "the skinny" explanation. Society's popular narrative mixes up emotions and feelings, acting like every feeling you have is somehow valid or accurate. That's a dangerous belief. On one side, men are told to suppress all emotions, while women are encouraged to feel everything—sometimes under the guise of "intuition." From a brain-based perspective, both of these extremes are a problem.

Emotions are physiological reactions—signals from your body to your brain.[3] They can be triggered by external stimuli or by thoughts and memories. They're natural and necessary, and sometimes you absolutely have to suppress them in high-pressure situations. But letting those emotions rot inside you without an outlet or becoming unaware that you're even experiencing them? That's where the damage starts.

Feelings, on the other hand, are stories (interpretations) your mind creates about those emotions.[4] They're shaped by your thoughts, beliefs, and past experiences—and here's the thing: Feelings aren't always rooted in reality. Research shows how our brain can misjudge situations and create distorted interpretations.[5] Your brain is capable of spinning all kinds of false narratives, so you need to be skeptical of what you feel. Don't trust every feeling—challenge it, test it, and become aware that your brain could definitely be f*cking with you.

The Cost of Suppressing Emotions: A Ticking Time Bomb

Let's talk about what happens when you suppress dark emotions like anger, jealousy, and resentment. Whether you're doing it consciously or not, that suppression is going to cost you—big time.

Here's the ugly truth: Research shows that chronic emotional suppression is linked to higher levels of anxiety, depression, and even physical health problems.[6] You might have to hold it together at work or in critical situations—I get that. But ignoring and suppressing those emotions altogether? That's where the real damage happens.

And let's be honest, men are especially prone to this. Society tells men that being a tough bad*ss means keeping your emotions in check at all times. Otherwise, you'll be perceived as weak and incompetent. There's a problem with that premise for any human being. It results in disconnection, numbness, and losing touch with what's really going on inside you. It also means it's only a matter of time before you go from zero to a hundred in a split second. Suppression isn't some badge of honor—it's a ticking time bomb.

Many people suppress dark emotions until they're pushed too far because they don't know how to set boundaries. They think they can handle anything, until they snap.

I hear it all the time with both men and women: "I can take a lot, but watch out if I'm pushed too far!" That's not mastery—that's often a lack of assertiveness and poor boundaries. Don't let that be you. If you're waiting for someone to push you over the edge, you're not in control of your brain.

Chronic suppression and repression of emotions physically alter your brain and nervous system.[7] Like it or not, suppressing emotions cranks up stress hormones like cortisol, kills brain cells, screws with your memory, and basically hijacks your prefrontal cortex (a.k.a. your thinking center).[8] The fallout? Anxiety, depression, broken relationships, and sometimes a total collapse of your moral compass. When you keep shoving down your emotions, they'll find a way to leak out—often in ways that mess up your life, your integrity, and everything you care about.

This hits both men and women. I know it firsthand: I grew up in trauma, and at one point, I was so emotionally shut down that I got misdiagnosed with a schizoid personality disorder. I was flat-lined—no highs, no lows, just numb. That is how I lived my life, until I knew better.

Here's what I tell my clients: Just because you've been given a diagnosis doesn't mean you actually have that disorder. Chronic emotional suppression and trauma can look like something else entirely.[9] It might appear like you have a mental health illness or personality disorder, but that doesn't mean it's necessarily true. You are more complex than that.

My point is that it's mandatory to integrate your emotions, embody them, regulate them, and find healthy outlets to express them. If you don't, the consequences stack up—immune system issues, chronic pain, digestive problems, insomnia, and so much more.[10]

For me, drumming is my go-to outlet for releasing stress and pent-up emotions. It's physical, it's intense, and it lets me purge all that toxic energy in a way that keeps me balanced. Body-based practices are seriously powerful for emotional release and self-regulation.[11] You need to find what works for you. Fast, high-energy activities can be great tension-busters, but watch out—if you're not careful, tension in the body can create more stress. The goal is to find a physical activity (preferably a mind-body practice) that's both powerful and relaxing. You've got to find something that allows you to face your dark emotions, integrate, and express them so you can experience a vast array of positive emotions. Dark emotions are just part of the human experience. Suppressing them doesn't make them vanish. They resurface as resentment or other toxic behaviors down the road.

Real-World Emotional Misinterpretation

If you're used to suppressing emotions, you might find yourself numb, checked out, and completely disconnected from what's happening in your body. On the flip side, if you're constantly getting lost in your feelings—emotionally dysregulated and all over the place—you're probably not even recognizing the difference between emotions and feelings. Both situations can lead to extreme, often irrational, reactions.

Have you ever experienced one of the following?
1. Instantly, you had a bad feeling about someone you didn't know.
2. Felt like someone was disrespecting you.
3. Convinced yourself that someone didn't love you.
4. Thought someone was looking for a fight.
5. Felt your life was in danger when it wasn't.

These are all subjective interpretations—not necessarily grounded in reality. That might sting, especially if you've been conditioned to "trust your feelings" and believe they're always valid. Cognitive biases like those described by Kahneman and Tversky (1979) show that our interpretations are often way off, leading us to misread social cues and interactions.[12]

I see this misinterpretation more often in women than men. Women are often encouraged to feel their way through life, with "intuition" held up as a guiding principle. That's a dangerous game. Without discernment between emotions and feelings, you'll be prone to see the world through a broken lens. Even the most insignificant iota of emotion will be interpreted as the truth of the situation but not based in reality. That places you in a vulnerable position where you have very little control over external or internal experiences.

When it comes to leadership, many leaders in society have been conditioned to suppress their emotions to such an extent that they lose touch with what it means to be fully human. They become disengaged, like walking bobbleheads, as their brains practically sever the connection between their heads and bodies to excel in their roles. This detachment is a breeding ground for moral corruption because if you don't fully experience emotions, your integrity is bound to be compromised. I'm not saying this to be disrespectful; it's simply the truth, and I wouldn't wish this on anyone. To avoid this fate, you must discern the difference between emotions and feelings and learn how to process and integrate them effectively.

How Do Misinterpreted "Feelings" Play out in Real Life?

Let me give you an example. I worked with a highly successful female doctor who was stuck in a cycle of workplace abuse and harassment. By the time she found me, her brain was jammed in overdrive. She was constantly triggered by the smallest situations and most insignificant comments from others. She was deep in a victim mentality, feeling powerless in her interactions with others. She was spiraling into resentment, bitterness, and total isolation—a textbook case of someone being trapped in victimhood without the skills needed to escape. One of the most disempowering mindsets you can have is believing you're at the mercy of what happens to you.

Her brain was feeding her lies, convincing her that her feelings were facts. For example, she valued excellence, integrity, and work ethic—admirable traits that fueled her success. But when her boss gave her critical feedback, her brain registered it as a full-blown threat, triggering old trauma and sending her from zero to a hundred in seconds. Her brain twisted the situation into a claim of harassment and abuse, and she spiraled into hyper-reactive thoughts like:

- How dare they do that to me!
- Why does this always happen to me?
- Why is nothing I do ever good enough?
- I hate my life.

The core issue? Her hyperactive amygdala—the brain's fear center—was triggering a flood of emotional reactivity, hijacking her ability to think clearly and respond rationally.[13]

But once she learned to separate her emotions (fear) from her interpretations (disrespect), she found stability. Over time, she learned how to release pent-up toxic energy, integrate those dark emotions, and feed her soul so she could thrive again. She is now on her way to becoming an exceptional leader in her field!

I want to highlight that it's your personal responsibility not to live your life at the mercy of other people or external circumstances. If you do, you've got a one-way ticket to misery and powerlessness. You have to take responsibility for what's happening in your own brain. Challenge your feelings, integrate your dark emotions, and embrace the positive ones as often as possible. The key is learning how to respond instead of react.

The R.E.S.T. Method: Regaining Control of Your Brain

By now, you know how easily your brain can hijack your emotions, leaving you reactive, disempowered, disengaged, and at the mercy of whatever life throws at you. If you're conditioned to trigger emotionally and blame others—*They shouldn't have said that, They shouldn't have done that,* or *They shouldn't have looked at me like that*—let's get one thing straight: It's not them. It's you. More specifically, it's your brain misfiring.

What's liberating is that once you know what's really happening, you can take back control. I'm going to show you a technique you need to master so you're no longer at the mercy of what others say or how emotional triggers hijack you. This method is simple but powerful—it's called the R.E.S.T. Method, a unique approach I've been developing specifically for managing tough situations, high stress, and overwhelming emotions. The R.E.S.T. method can be used when facing tough conversations or preparing for a high-stress situation. I use it all the time—whether writing, talking to a client, or making a critical decision. The R.E.S.T. method is my go-to tool. It stands for Reset, Evaluate, Set Intentions, and Take Action.

Once you've mastered these four steps, they become quick and seamless—allowing you to stay in control instead of getting hijacked by emotional triggers.

Here's how it works:

1. **Reset:** Start by resetting your nervous system using the physiological sigh. This technique, popularized by Dr. Andrew Huberman, is simple yet incredibly effective. Take two deep breaths in—one long, one short—followed by a long exhale. Repeat two or three times. It quickly calms your nervous system and helps you regain control over your cognitive processes.[14]

2. **Evaluate:** Briefly analyze the situation. What are the facts? Don't go down a rabbit hole—keep it simple. For example: *I'm about to have a challenging conversation*, or *I'm entering a potentially stressful situation*. Stick to the facts. This step activates your prefrontal cortex—the part of your brain responsible for logical reasoning and impulse control—helping you detach from the emotional narrative your brain might be creating.[15]

3. **Set Intentions:** Ask yourself, *Is what I'm about to do bringing me closer to or further away from what I want?* You need a clear intention. Don't let others control the narrative—take charge of your own. This step engages your brain's goal-oriented circuits and primes your brain to focus on actions and stimuli that align with your objectives.[16]

4. **Take Action:** With clarity, move forward with purpose. You've reset your system, evaluated the facts, and aligned your intentions. Now, take action from a place of control. This step reinforces self-directed neuroplasticity—rewiring your brain to favor emotional regulation and purposeful behavior.[17]

Mastering the R.E.S.T. method will make this process feel natural, almost automatic. You'll find yourself in control, no longer at the mercy of external triggers or emotional reactions.

If you've got a high-stress job, practice the R.E.S.T. method before heading home or when dealing with tense situations. This is your responsibility. This is where your power lies.

And if you think this sounds like too much work, let me be clear: suffering is a lot more work. This method takes seconds—maybe a minute—but it's incredibly effective.

A Brain-Based Explanation for Why the R.E.S.T. Method Works

The R.E.S.T. method isn't some fluffy quick fix—it's grounded in applied neuroscience. Here's why it works:

1. **Reset: Activating the Parasympathetic Nervous System:** The first step, Reset, taps into the power of the physiological sigh to engage your parasympathetic nervous system—the part that chills you out. Research shows that controlled breathing techniques like this one activate your vagus nerve, which is the key player in calming both your body and mind.[18] By taking those controlled breaths, you quiet your sympathetic nervous system (the "fight-or-flight" mode) and reset your emotional state. This primes your brain for clear thinking and stops emotional hijacking before it takes over.

2. **Evaluate: Engaging the Prefrontal Cortex:** When you evaluate the facts consciously, you shift activity away from the emotional fear-based amygdala and back to the logical prefrontal cortex. Under stress, your prefrontal cortex—the part that handles logical reasoning—takes a backseat, leading to impulsive, emotion-driven decisions.[19] Evaluating the facts lets you take back control, cutting through cognitive distortions and focusing on what's objectively true instead of getting swept up in emotional noise.

3. **Set Intentions: Aligning with Your Goals and Values:** Setting clear intentions is more than just a mental exercise—it's a way to activate your brain's reward system. When your actions align with your goals and values, your brain's circuits get primed to reinforce positive behavior, helping you filter out distractions and zero in on what actually matters.[20] This keeps you locked in on your objectives instead of getting thrown off course by external nonsense.

4. **Take Action: Strengthening Self-Directed Neuroplasticity:** Every time you take intentional action, you're rewiring your brain. Research has established that behavior modification can lead to systematic changes in brain function, showing that self-directed neuroplasticity is the real deal.[21] When you choose to respond instead of react, you build new neural pathways that favor emotional regulation and intentional decision-making. Over time, this makes it easier for your brain to default to controlled, deliberate responses instead of falling back into old, destructive patterns.

The Write-to-Right Method: Releasing Pent-Up Emotions

Now, let's dive into an unconventional yet powerful method for offloading pent-up emotions: the Write-to-Right method, or as I like to call it, the "Dear Motherf*cker" exercise. It's straightforward and highly effective.

1. **Step 1:** Grab a pen and paper (yes, actual paper—no computers or digital shortcuts). Visualize the person or situation that's been gnawing at you.

2. **Step 2:** At the top of the page, write: *Dear Motherf*cker*, and then pour out every ounce of that dark, nasty emotion you've been bottling up. Don't hold back—no censoring, no politeness. Let all the rage, frustration, and resentment spill onto that page. Say all the things you've been conditioned not to say, think, feel or experience. Let it all out. Don't stop until you have nothing else to say.

3. **Step 3:** Once you're done, rip it up into tiny pieces and get rid of it. This exercise is for your eyes and your soul only.

If this feels uncomfortable because it's not how you typically express yourself—guess what? You probably need it the most. Releasing those emotions you've been told you "shouldn't feel" is incredibly liberating. Every client who's tried this has experienced immediate relief. Yes, it's unconventional, but it works.

A Brain-Based Explanation for Why the Write-to-Right Method Works

The Write-to-Right method is rooted in the principles of emotional regulation, cognitive control, and cathartic release:

1. **Emotional Regulation: Releasing Pent-Up Energy:** When intense emotions like anger or frustration build up, your brain triggers stress hormones like cortisol and adrenaline. If unexpressed, these emotions can stay stuck in your system, leading to chronic stress and even physical health problems. Research shows that expressive writing offers a controlled outlet, signaling to your brain that it can let go of this toxic energy.[22]
2. **Engaging the Prefrontal Cortex: Gaining Cognitive Control:** Writing down your thoughts shifts activity from the reactive amygdala to the logical prefrontal cortex, allowing you to transform raw emotional energy into something manageable. This shift helps you gain clarity and perspective.[23]
3. **Cathartic Release: Clearing Emotional and Mental Clutter:** Writing unfiltered thoughts is a form of catharsis—an emotional release that brings psychological relief.[24] The act of tearing up the paper afterward symbolizes releasing the emotional burden, signaling to your brain that these emotions no longer hold power over you.

4. **Disrupting Rumination: Breaking Negative Feedback Loops:** The Write-to-Right method disrupts rumination by externalizing repetitive negative thoughts. Once those thoughts are on paper, they lose their power, breaking the cycle of mental clutter.[25]
5. **Creating a Sense of Agency: Empowering Your Soul:** This exercise gives you control over how you process difficult emotions. You're training your brain to understand that you are in charge—not the emotions. Research on neuroplasticity shows that intentional practices like this reinforce cognitive control and foster resilience.[25]

Soul Care vs. Self-Care: Feeding the Fire Within

Now, let's talk about soul care—something far more intentional, powerful, and essential than self-care.

Self-care is about addressing your basic needs—like getting massages, taking vacations, or eating healthy. Soul care, on the other hand, is about feeding the fire that burns within you. It's what fortifies your soul and gives it the strength to command your brain rather than letting it run wild. Research shows that engaging in activities aligned with your core values leads to deeper, more sustained well-being.[27]

Here's the truth: The things that feed our souls are often a little weird. They resonate deeply, even if they make no sense to others. For me, drumming has been my passion since I was 12. It might not make logical sense to anyone else, but it has always fed my soul.

Ignoring what feeds your soul leads to suffering.

You can try to convince yourself that it doesn't matter, but you'd be lying to yourself. Research highlights how pursuing what truly resonates with your authentic self enhances motivation and long-term fulfillment.[28]

Maybe you're into something unconventional—like painting rocks or building birdhouses. Society might label it as "weird," especially if it doesn't make you money. But if you neglect what lights you up, you'll pay the price. Your soul will wither, resentment will build, and you'll lose that fire within you. Engaging in creative pursuits, even those deemed unconventional, has been shown to protect against burnout and enhance mental health.[29]

You have to intentionally build your soul if you want to sustain personal excellence. This isn't optional.

Remember, the stronger your soul, the easier it is to command your brain to work in your favor. That's key.

And here's the thing: Soul care isn't always about easy or relaxing activities. Your soul craves challenges. It thrives on doing hard things because challenges build self-respect. Ignoring what your soul values is a direct act of self-disrespect.

It's not impressive to do everything except what your soul craves. That's a surefire way to end up resentful, miserable, and eventually depressed. Take a moment to ask yourself what your soul truly desires—what you love that you've been neglecting—and make a conscious choice to move in that direction. We'll dive deeper into this in the chapters to come.

Chapter 3 Takeaways

Don'ts:

- **Don't Suppress Your Emotions.** Suppressing dark emotions like anger, jealousy, and resentment is a fast track to disconnection and misery. You might need to keep it together sometimes, but neglecting healthy outlets is a recipe for long-term disaster.
- **Don't Mistake Feelings for Facts.** Feelings are not facts. Just because you feel something doesn't make it true. Learn to separate what's real from the story your brain is spinning.
- **Don't Ignore What Fuels Your Soul.** Dismissing your passions because they don't "make sense" is soul-crushing. Ignore what truly lights you up, and you'll end up bitter, resentful, and empty.

- **Don't Wait Until You Snap.** Resilience isn't about gritting your teeth until you crack. It's about setting boundaries and taking control before everything spirals out of control.

Do's:
- **Do Integrate and Express Dark Emotions.** Face your shadows head-on. Acknowledge the dark emotions, process them, and release them before they poison your body and life.
- **Do Challenge Your Feelings.** Question everything, especially when you're emotional. Feelings are often misleading—stick to the facts and take back control.
- **Do Prioritize Soul Care *and* Self-Care.** You need both. Self-care is the obvious, but feed the passions that ignite your inner fire, no matter how unconventional. That's what keeps your soul alive.
- **Do Embrace Challenges for Soul Growth.** Your soul thrives on doing hard things. It's not about comfort—it's about pushing yourself, building self-respect, and living aligned with your true values.

Chapter 3 Summary: Mastering Both Your Brain and Your Soul

Chapter 3 is all about mastering both your brain and your soul. Optimizing brain function sharpens your focus, decision-making, and productivity. But that's only one side of the coin. Building a formidable soul means aligning your actions with what truly matters—your core values and passions, and integrating every aspect of yourself, even the dark, messy parts. That's how you build a soul strong enough to command your brain, not the other way around.

The real problem? Society's got people twisted about emotions and feelings: emotions are physiological signals; feelings are stories your brain tells you. Most people confuse the two and end up emotionally unstable or trapped in victimhood. This chapter dived into why you need to integrate dark emotions in healthy ways and challenge your feelings instead of taking them at face value.

To help you get there, I introduce two powerhouse techniques: the R.E.S.T. method for taking back control in stressful situations and the "Dear Motherf*cker" exercise for dumping emotional baggage. Both are raw, effective, and designed to give you back the reins instead of letting your emotions run wild.

The bottom line? Self-care isn't enough—you need soul care. Your soul craves challenges, growth, and the stuff that truly lights you up. Ignore that, and you'll end up stuck in resentment, burnout, and regret. This chapter lays the foundation for understanding that mastering your brain is crucial, but building a formidable soul is non-negotiable if you want real success and fulfillment.

Myth 3: Men naturally manage stress better than women.

Truth: Studies show that men and women process stress differently, but men are not inherently better at handling it (Kudielka et al., 2005). Society, culture, community, and environment all play a role in how you interpret stress. The key is developing stress management tools that are specific to your brain, mind, body, and soul, regardless of gender.

CHAPTER 4

Conquering Inner Chaos

*"The suicidal mind state is one of profound disconnection.
It is an altered state of reality."*
–Dr. Shauna Springer

This is worth repeating: The inner chaos and turmoil you're experiencing aren't necessarily caused by external circumstances. It's easy to think that if life weren't so damn difficult—if challenges, adversity, and stress didn't keep piling up—you wouldn't have to deal with anxiety, agitation, confusion, and overwhelm. You'd be thriving and always on top of your game!

But the reality is, outer chaos often mirrors inner chaos.

There's more to it than that. An overactive or underactive brain and nervous system can cause intense mental, emotional, physical, and spiritual suffering. It amplifies the tension and disturbances within your body, mind, and soul, manifesting as anxiety, depression, confusion, and other uncomfortable experiences tied to unresolved trauma and chronic stress. This isn't about dismissing the chaos in your life or the world. Life can be chaotic. The world can feel chaotic. But that doesn't mean you're at the mercy of external events forever. There are tangible ways to mitigate this suffering and transform it into personal power. And believe it or not, these methods can be both pleasurable and meaningful.

In this chapter, I'll walk you through another brain-based perspective involving what might be causing your inner chaos and how to conquer it to create more peace and fulfillment. We'll explore the five primary areas of the brain impacted by trauma, the importance of both top-down and bottom-up techniques, why embracing an Outlier Mindset is essential, and the value of applied rhythmic entrainment. It sounds like a lot, but I promise to tie it all together. If you're dealing with inner chaos, the insights in this chapter can free your soul from pain so you can experience more joy, inner peace, and fulfillment—because that's what you deserve.

Your Brain Is Under Siege

Taking responsibility for your inner chaos is hard—especially if you've got to deal with a whole lot of bullshit happening around you. But here's the thing: When your brain is under siege from external threats—whether real or perceived—it will likely start to misfire and malfunction. You might think you have no control, but once again, you have to challenge your brain.

To help you understand what's really going on, I'll break down the five primary areas of the brain impacted by traumatic stress. Understanding this will cut through self-blame and destroy the false belief that your inner turmoil is due to mental weakness or a moral deficiency. This knowledge is crucial for sustaining personal excellence and achieving any kind of meaningful change.

Even if you think this doesn't apply to you, remember: your brain has likely been affected by the collective trauma of the COVID pandemic, whether you realize it or not. Full credit goes to clinical psychologist Dr. Jennifer Sweeton for providing research and education that support these findings.[1]

I'll keep it concise, but here are the five primary areas of the brain affected by trauma:

1. **The Amygdala – Your Fear Center**: This area gets a lot of attention for good reason. It evaluates danger, identifies threats, and prepares your brain and body for action—the fight, flight, freeze, or flop response. It operates outside your conscious control, so it can misfire

even when there's no real threat. Trauma and chronic stress can cause this area to be overactive, leading to heightened reactions to perceived threats that aren't actually there.[2] Deactivating this area is necessary to reduce trauma-triggered reactivity and the inner chaos it fuels.

2. **The Hippocampus - Your Memory Center:** The hippocampus is responsible for explicit, declarative, and autobiographical memories —those you can consciously recall. Under intense stress or trauma, the hippocampus can shrink and become less active, leading to memory issues.[3] This is why memories formed during stress may be distorted. The hippocampus closely communicates with the amygdala, which evaluates danger based on past experiences. If the hippocampus is compromised, it may relay incorrect information to the amygdala, triggering inaccurate fear and anxiety responses, distorted memories, impaired learning, and even relationship challenges.[2] Just because your memories feel vivid and accurate doesn't mean they're entirely based on facts.

3. **The Insula - Your Interoception Center:** The insula doesn't get enough attention, but it deserves the spotlight. It's responsible for proprioception—your sense of balance and body awareness. It's also responsible for interoception, which is your ability to feel internal experiences and connect to your inner sensations. For example, your ability to accurately assess when you're feeling hungry or when you experience physical sensations in your body. When it functions properly, it helps you identify and regulate emotions. But when it's dysregulated due to trauma or chronic stress, it disrupts your ability to feel your body's physiological responses to emotions.[4] You might feel like your head is disconnected from your body. As I mentioned in the last chapter. I see this frequently with my male clients. They are courageous, intelligent and successful, yet they've suppressed their emotions for so long they've become emotionally unavailable.

On the flip side, women often experience hypersensitivity in this area, mistaking it for intuition or gut feelings that might not be accurate. Both these situations are largely due to a dysregulated insula. The more regulated this area is, the less you'll suffer from emotional outbursts, and the safer you'll feel in your body.

4. **The Prefrontal Cortex – Your Thinking Center:** Located in the front part of your brain, the prefrontal cortex is responsible for decision-making, problem-solving, concentration, empathy, self-awareness, and self-regulation. When you experience trauma or chronic stress, this area can become underactive, making it difficult to concentrate, connect with others, or make effective decisions.[5] This is why you might find yourself making destructive choices without fully realizing what you're doing. Activating this area is essential if you want to enhance focus, decision-making, connection, and self-awareness—all of which are necessary for achieving greatness and living the life you want.

5. **The Anterior Cingulate Cortex – Your Self-Regulation Center:** This area is crucial for self-regulation and managing conflicting thoughts and emotions. If you've experienced trauma, chronic stress, or suppressed anger and anxiety, this area is likely underactive or weakened.[6] As a result, you may struggle to regulate painful emotions and thoughts, leading to more inner chaos. Activating this region helps reduce stress and manage distressing emotions and thoughts more effectively.

Can you see my point about not being fully aware of how your brain (or someone else's brain) is functioning? It's basically impossible to tell. Do you have to memorize the details of these areas to master your brain? No. You just need to be aware that these are the five primary brain areas affected by trauma and chronic stress. Understanding this should lift the weight of self-blame and destroy the belief that your struggles are due to weakness or lack of willpower.

This is real, and it's based on solid science. The good news? You can learn to stack the odds in your favor and take back control of your brain.

Top-Down and Bottom-Up Strategies: The Key to Retraining Your Brain

Once you understand what it takes to master your brain and have the right tools in place, you're in a position of power. It doesn't mean you won't face challenges, but it does mean you'll be better equipped to handle them. Sustained personal excellence, success, and fulfillment require a fully integrated, well-connected, and resilient brain. This is where self-directed neuroplasticity comes into play.

Top-down and bottom-up techniques are essential for retraining your brain (especially the areas I just mentioned) to work in your favor. Let's break these techniques down.

1. **Top-Down Techniques: Using Your Mind to Change Your Brain:** Top-down techniques involve consciously directing your thoughts to influence higher cortical areas of your brain. These methods strengthen the prefrontal cortex, which is responsible for self-regulation and executive functions. Common top-down techniques include cognitive-behavioral therapy (CBT), mindfulness, positive affirmations, visualization, psychotherapy, and many other methods that use your mind to change your brain. Studies have found these methods help create lasting changes in your brain's structure and function by reinforcing neural pathways that support positive behavior and thought patterns.[7]
2. **Bottom-Up Techniques: Using Your Body to Retrain Your Brain:** Bottom-up techniques target lower and mid-level brain regions like the limbic system, which includes the amygdala, hippocampus, insula, and brainstem. These areas control emotional regulation, survival instincts, and automatic responses. Bottom-up approaches

include rhythmic breathing, physical exercise, yoga, dance, sensory integration activities, and other mind-body practices. These methods regulate your body's physiological responses, making it easier to achieve emotional stability and mental clarity.[8]

Most people rely solely on top-down techniques and neglect the importance of bottom-up strategies. You need both. It's impossible to thrive by using only your mind to overcome adversity without retraining the lower and mid-level areas of your brain. You have to learn how to experience your body and your inner sensations. This is the missing piece in most personal development and mental health approaches.[9]

By integrating both top-down and bottom-up techniques, you're laying the groundwork for truly transformative change, which is essential, especially if you want to adopt the Outlier Mindset—a mindset that pushes beyond conventional limits and challenges the norms that hold most people back.

The Outlier Mindset: Thinking Beyond the Norm

The Outlier Mindset is more than just an attitude; it's a unique mental framework that empowers you to break free from conventional thinking and tap into the limitless potential of your brain and soul. It's a perspective that embraces the unconventional, welcoming innovation and adaptability in the face of challenges. The Outlier Mindset requires you to often think, act, and live outside societal norms because if you want exceptional results, you must be willing to do what the average person won't.[10]

This mindset involves a commitment to creativity, continuous learning, and an unwavering determination to forge your own path—no matter how many people tell you it can't be done. It's about recognizing that societal norms and traditions often cater to mediocrity, and if you're reading this, you're not interested in living a mediocre life. You're here because you're pursuing personal greatness, and that requires thinking and acting differently from the masses.

From the moment we're born, society imposes countless rules, expectations, and limitations on us. We're taught to think within the confines of what's deemed "acceptable" or "normal," and anyone who dares to step outside of that box is labeled as rebellious, weird, or even crazy. But here's the truth: Every major breakthrough—whether in science, art, business, or personal development—came from someone who refused to accept the status quo. The greatest innovators, leaders, and visionaries all share this Outlier Mindset.[11] They're the ones who questioned what everyone else blindly accepted, who found new solutions where others only saw dead ends.

But embracing this mindset isn't just about going against the grain for the sake of it. It's about recognizing that standard approaches often lead to standard results. If you want extraordinary outcomes in your life—whether that's in your career, relationships, health, or personal growth—you need to be willing to challenge conventional wisdom and adopt strategies that others might not even consider.

How the Outlier Mindset Fuels Your Personal Excellence

The Outlier Mindset is crucial for conquering inner chaos because it enables you to approach challenges with a perspective that most people don't even realize exists. For instance, when most people face anxiety or stress, they rely solely on mainstream methods like talk therapy or medication. While those methods have their place, they're often not enough. The Outlier Mindset allows you to explore unconventional solutions—like music as medicine and applied rhythmic entrainment—which most people overlook or dismiss because they fall outside the standard approach. I'll discuss more about this shortly.

I've already introduced you to several techniques and philosophies that deviate from the norm. You'll notice that I'm not here to offer cookie-cutter advice or recycled self-help strategies. Instead, I'm providing you with tools that work but aren't always considered mainstream. Why? Because if you want more than average results, you need more than average methods.

The Outlier Mindset pushes you to continuously evolve, to seek out what actually works rather than what's simply popular. This mindset means being willing to experiment, to fail, and to learn from those failures without losing momentum. It's about embracing complexity and understanding that growth often requires going through discomfort and doing things that others won't even try.

One of the biggest barriers to adopting the Outlier Mindset is the fear of judgment. People who live by conventional standards often won't understand your decisions or your approach to life. They might tell you that you're wrong, misguided, or unrealistic. But here's the thing: those people are usually stuck in their own limiting beliefs. They're living by the rules that society laid out for them, and they can't see beyond that.

Attracting Relationships That Align with Your Path

When you fully embrace the Outlier Mindset, you don't just attract unconventional success—you also draw in relationships that reflect your true values and goals. This mindset creates a magnetic force that pulls in people who resonate with your vision and energy. Whether in business, friendship, or even love, living authentically opens the door to deep, meaningful connections that support your journey.

Sometimes, that might even include attracting a soulmate who mirrors your commitment to growth, creativity, and living life on your terms. When you align with your purpose and stay true to your path, you naturally draw in the kind of relationships that elevate and inspire you—both personally and professionally.

To truly harness the power of the Outlier Mindset, you need to develop an unshakable belief in your own path, even when others doubt you. This means trusting that you have the inner resources and creativity to figure things out, even when the way forward isn't clear. It's about having the courage to make decisions based on what aligns with your core values and goals, not what society tells you is "right" or "acceptable."

The Outlier Mindset also involves recognizing that the limitations placed on you by society, culture, or even your past experiences are often illusions. Yes, challenges are real, and yes, obstacles can be difficult—but they're not insurmountable. By thinking outside the norm, you can find solutions that others would never even consider.

For example, while traditional methods for managing anxiety might focus on cognitive strategies alone, the Outlier Mindset encourages you to incorporate holistic and body-based techniques like drumming, rhythmic movement, and somatic practices. These methods might seem unconventional to some, but they're rooted in solid neuroscience and have been used for centuries across cultures to heal and transform.[12]

When you break free from the confines of mainstream thinking, you unlock possibilities that others don't even realize exist. This is how you move from simply managing your chaos to mastering it.

Cultivating the Courage to Be Different

One of the most important qualities of the Outlier Mindset is the courage to be different. It takes guts to go against the grain, to pursue methods that aren't widely accepted, and to stand firm in your choices even when others criticize or doubt you. But that's exactly what's required if you want to live an extraordinary life.

Remember, most people settle for average because it's safe and socially reinforced. But you're not here to be average. You're here to excel, to push boundaries, and to create a life that's uniquely yours. That's why the Outlier Mindset is non-negotiable. It's the mental framework that allows you to transcend societal limitations and achieve results that most people can only dream of.

If you're serious about conquering inner chaos and achieving greatness, you have to be willing to adopt the Outlier Mindset in every aspect of your life. That includes being open to unconventional approaches such as applied rhythmic entrainment. It might not be the first thing that comes to mind when you think about mental and emotional well-being, but that's precisely why it works. It's different; it's effective, and it taps into the brain and body's innate ability to heal and transform.

Applied Rhythmic Entrainment: Syncing Your Brain and Body

Applied rhythmic entrainment refers to the neurophysiological synchronization that happens when your brain and body align with an external rhythm, like music or drumbeats.[13] Using music as medicine isn't a new concept—it's been practiced for centuries across cultures.[14] However, applying drumming as a tool to retrain the brain is a relatively new breakthrough in scientific literature.

Modern science now supports what many ancient traditions have always known: rhythmic-based approaches are highly effective for mental health, stress reduction, and overall well-being. Research shows that rhythmic entrainment can modulate brain wave patterns, regulate the autonomic nervous system, and promote emotional balance.[15]

Yet, despite the evidence, there are still few therapeutic approaches that fully leverage rhythm. As a drummer, you can imagine how shocked I was by this realization. It became a valuable nudge in the right direction during my academic pursuit. That's why I devoted significant time during my higher education to researching and documenting everything I could find on the neuroscience and clinical application of drumming.

This research led to the development of Neuro-Rhythmic Trauma Therapy (NRTT), a method I created to help those dealing with PTSD and unresolved trauma. While this book isn't focused on trauma recovery, I'd be doing you a disservice if I didn't introduce how applied rhythmic entrainment can help you conquer inner chaos and reconnect with your body.

But to be clear, there is no way I can accurately explain exactly how you will experience rhythmic techniques in your brain, body, mind, or soul! Some techniques—especially rhythm-based ones—can't be fully captured through written words alone. Describing a musical or rhythmic process in a book is like trying to teach someone to dance using only text. It's possible, but it's nowhere near as effective as actually seeing it in action and feeling it in your body. I can, however, confidently tell you that research supports that experiential learning—especially through rhythm—engages multiple sensory modalities, enhancing neuroplasticity and making therapeutic effects more potent.[16] You need to fully experience applied rhythmic entrainment to really grasp its full impact, but for now, I will try to help you understand how it works to retrain your brain and nervous system.

The Science Behind Applied Rhythmic Entrainment

There's something primal about how our brains respond to rhythm. Applied rhythmic entrainment taps into this by syncing your brain and body to an external beat—like music or drum patterns. When your sensory and motor systems lock into that rhythm, something incredible happens: Your brainwaves shift. Those chaotic, overactive brain states associated with stress and anxiety? They start to settle down.[17]

Here's how it works: Your brain operates on different frequencies depending on your mental state. When you're anxious or stressed, your brain fires off high-frequency beta waves, keeping you in a heightened state of alertness. But when you engage in rhythmic activities like drumming, your brainwaves shift toward more relaxed frequencies, such as alpha and theta waves, which are linked to calm, creativity, and deep focus.[19]

Drumming isn't just about banging on some skins—it's about retraining your brain, specifically targeting lower to mid-level areas of your brain without relying on "thinking" your way out of dysregulation. To top it off, when you drum, both hemispheres of your brain get activated, forging new neural connections that enhance motor coordination, cognitive function, and emotional regulation.[20] This is especially crucial if you're dealing with trauma, anxiety, or depression because rhythmic stimulation can break those toxic loops your brain gets stuck in.

Think of it this way: Your brain is like a looping playlist stuck on repeat, replaying the same thoughts, feelings, and reactions over and over again. Rhythmic entrainment disrupts that loop, helping you reset and redirect your mental and emotional patterns.

Once again, here's where the magic happens—self-directed neuroplasticity. This is worth repeating: Your brain is constantly reshaping itself based on your experiences, habits, and actions. Rhythmic exercises like drumming leverage this natural capacity by forming healthier neural connections. Scientific studies confirm that repetitive rhythmic activities not only improve mood and attention but also enhance social connection and empathy.[21] It's no surprise that cultures have used drumming for thousands of years to heal, connect, and transform.[22]

Grounding and Stabilizing Through Rhythm

Let's not forget about the body in all this. Rhythmic techniques engage both your sensory and motor systems, grounding you in the present moment. When your nervous system is out of whack—whether it's over-activated from stress or numbed from dissociation—rhythm is a powerful way to bring it back into balance. Research indicates that rhythmic activities help regulate the autonomic nervous system, lower cortisol levels, and ultimately reduce stress.[23]

As noted previously, plenty of scientific data has revealed that drumming can reduce symptoms of anxiety, depression, and PTSD by promoting rhythmic synchronization in the brain and body.[24] Before you even think about dismissing it as just another "technique," I'm challenging you to experience it for yourself. You'll be surprised at how quickly and effectively it shifts your mental and emotional state.

Like I said before, you won't fully grasp the power of these techniques just by reading about them. You have to experience it. That's why **I've included a QR code at the end of this chapter, linking you to two specific rhythmic strategies.** The Four-Minute Habit is designed to reduce anxiety in real-time, and the Mantra of Intrigue introduces you to a rhythmic meditation practice that will start retraining your brain for inner peace. You might be skeptical at first—that's fine. But trust me, these methods are practical, pleasurable, and they flat-out work.

Chapter 4 Takeaways

Don'ts:

- **Don't Ignore Your Body.** Trying to think your way out of inner chaos without addressing your body's signals is ineffective. Neglecting bottom-up techniques can leave your nervous system in a state of constant dysregulation.
- **Don't Overlook the Impact of Trauma.** Inner chaos isn't always about mental weakness—it's often rooted in how trauma has altered your brain. Ignoring this reality only adds to self-blame and frustration.
- **Don't Settle for One-Size-Fits-All Solutions.** Mainstream methods may not always be enough. Relying solely on standard approaches can leave you stuck in unproductive cycles.

Do's:

- **Do Embrace Both Top-Down and Bottom-Up Approaches.** Rewiring your brain requires a combination of mental strategies and body-based practices. Integrating both is key to building resilience and reducing inner chaos.
- **Do Incorporate Rhythmic Techniques.** Methods like drumming and rhythmic movement are powerful tools for stabilizing your nervous system, calming your mind, and resetting your emotional state.
- **Do Recognize the Power of Self-Directed Neuroplasticity.** Your brain is constantly reshaping itself. Use techniques that intentionally guide this process toward healthier, more adaptive patterns.

Chapter 4 Summary: Conquering Inner Chaos

In this chapter, we examined the reality that inner chaos often reflects the state of our brain and nervous system. We explored the five primary areas of the brain impacted by trauma and chronic stress: the amygdala, hippocampus, insula, prefrontal cortex, and anterior cingulate cortex. Understanding how these areas affect our thoughts, emotions, and behaviors is key to reclaiming control and reducing inner turmoil.

I also discussed the importance of using both top-down and bottom-up strategies to rewire the brain. Top-down techniques focus on consciously directing your thoughts, while bottom-up methods leverage body-based practices like rhythmic entrainment to regulate the nervous system. Integrating the two approaches helps us build a more resilient, well-connected brain capable of handling life's challenges with greater ease.

I also emphasized the power of adopting an Outlier Mindset—thinking beyond societal norms to explore unconventional methods for conquering inner chaos. By embracing new unusual strategies, you tap into the brain's natural capacity for healing and transformation.

This chapter laid the groundwork for conquering your inner chaos, offering practical tools to help you regain control. By applying these strategies, you're taking real steps toward creating a more integrated, resilient brain—and that's mandatory for sustaining personal greatness!

Scan the QR Code to Access Two Specific Rhythmic Strategies & Extra Resources.

Myth 4: Sleep is for the weak.

Truth: Sacrificing sleep reduces mental sharpness and long-term performance. High performers who prioritize rest actually enhance their brain's ability to process information and make better decisions (Van Dogen et al., 2003). If you pride yourself on only needing a limited amount of sleep, I suggest you challenge that belief. Your brain is doing you a disservice, and eventually, you will pay the price with your health.

Myth 5: Drumming is just for musicians.

Truth: Drumming isn't just an artistic pursuit—it has profound effects on the brain and nervous system. Scientific studies show that drumming can improve cognitive function, enhance emotional regulation, and even support trauma recovery through rhythmic entrainment and brain-body synchronization. There's a wealth of scientific evidence to support these claims. If you're interested in a comprehensive list of references, feel free to reach out to me. In the meantime, explore the free training videos for this chapter to dive deeper into the neuroscience of drumming and its potential benefits.

Book Recommendation: For a deeper dive into the healing power of music, I recommend I Heard There Was a Secret Chord: Music as Medicine by Daniel Levitin (Penguin Random House, 2024).

CHAPTER 5

Creating Your Future Identity

*"You cannot be everything you want to be, but
you can be everything you are."*
–Jordan Peterson

If you're reading this book, it's probably safe to assume you understand the value of raising your standards. The fact that you were drawn to the term "Neuro-Mastery" tells me you're not the average person willing to let life pass by without pursuing personal growth. But have you ever considered elevating your standards by creating a new future identity through retraining your brain? I'm not talking about the outdated "fake it till you make it" method. I'm talking about rewiring your brain with new neural pathways that support the person you want to become.

Think of these neural pathways as a "survival of the busiest" system—whichever one you use most often is the one that stays in place.[1] That's what gets maintained. You can change your identity and personality by creating new neural pathways.[2] So, put yourself in the driver's seat because I'm about to give you a shortcut to creating your future identity.

The Power of Standards: Raise Them and Retrain Your Brain

I used to think that creating a new identity aligned with the person you want to become was nothing more than wishful thinking. I was never a fan of affirmations because pretending to be someone I wasn't didn't resonate with me. I don't subscribe to the belief that repeating something that isn't true will magically make it a reality. I'm all about taking action and doing the work.

Over time, though, I learned how to master an incredibly effective way to transform my identity while maintaining a sense of honesty and integrity. I've been using this method for over a decade, and I absolutely love it because it works so well. I've taught it to countless clients who have experienced life-changing results. Now, I realize that mastering the skill of creating your future identity is a must for anyone who wants to improve their life. It's about breaking free from the limitations of who you are today and stepping into the person you're capable of becoming.

From a brain-based perspective, you do have the power to shape your future self. It starts by consistently recognizing that your brain constantly processes your thoughts, beliefs, and behaviors associated with how you see yourself.[3] If you identify as lazy, unmotivated, anxious, or depressed, your brain will align those thoughts and actions to support that belief. But here's the good news: your conscious self (your soul) can override your brain's outdated perception of who you are by slowly integrating new words and concepts that inspire positive change.

The words you choose to describe yourself can influence your actions, which in turn influence your results, reinforcing the new identity you're creating. Don't fall for the lie that your personality or current identity is unchangeable. If you've found yourself thinking, *This is just who I am,* or *I've always been like this,* that's likely the problem. You're under no obligation to continue being who you've always been. You have every right to command your brain to align with the future identity of your choosing.

The trick is to attach new words to describe your future self so that your brain will align your thoughts and actions with the person you want to become. When you change the words that describe your identity, you're far more likely to change your behavior and, ultimately, the direction of your life.[4] Once again, you're going to get your brain to work for you instead of against you.

The Power of Three: A Top-Down Strategy

I want to give you a practical top-down strategy to make this possible. It's called the Power of Three.

Before you start this exercise, take a moment to write down three words that describe yourself right now—your current identity. Preferably, do this without looking ahead at any of the words listed. Be brutally honest with yourself about how you see yourself at this moment. For many of my clients, their initial words are often things like "frustrated," "stuck," "reactive," or "overwhelmed." That's the truth of their current reality.

Once you've done that, take a look at a list of identity words (also referred to as traits) and choose three words that capture the future identity you want to create.

Be sure that these words feel slightly out of reach—that's a good thing. Don't select words that you already feel comfortable with. Growth happens outside your comfort zone, so pick words that push you beyond where you are right now.

If words like "courageous," "passionate," and "optimistic" make you break a sweat, then those are likely the right ones for you. If words like "calm," "confident," and "sexy" make you nervous, choose those! This isn't the time to play small or settle for an identity that feels "safe." I'm giving you the framework to make this transformation possible, so trust yourself enough to aim high.

These words will guide you toward a future that aligns with your values and aspirations. Once you've identified your words, you can begin to envision your desired future self. Envisioning your future identity involves embodying the characteristics and traits of the person you want to become. Remember: Choose three words that truly capture the essence of your ideal future self. Keep in mind this will tie into other strategies, including the 90-Day Sprint Goal Framework later in the book.

Choose 3 Words To Describe Your Future Identity

In a world where it's easy to lose sight of who you are, it becomes essential for you to clarify your identity to avoid becoming someone you don't want to be. *Identify Your Own.*

Accomplished	Empowered	Optimistic
Active	Energetic	Organized
Adaptive	Enthusiastic	Outspoken
Affectionate	Exceptional	Passionate
Ambitious	Experienced	Patient
Attentive	Expressive	Peaceful
Authentic	Exuberant	Persistent
Awe-Inspiring	Fabulous	Proactive
Beautiful	Fearless	Professional
Bold	Focused	Protective
Brilliant	Forgiving	Rational
Calm	Generous	Relaxed
Candid	Genuine	Reliable
Charismatic	Happy	Resilient
Committed	Hardworking	Resourceful
Compassionate	Healthy	Respected
Competent	Heroic	Results-Oriented
Competitive	Honest	Romantic
Confident	Honourable	Selfless
Considerate	Iconic	Sexy
Courageous	Impactful	Spectacular
Creative	Influential	Strong
Decisive	Innovative	Structured
Dedicated	Insightful	Successful
Dependable	Inspiring	Sympathetic
Determined	Intuitive	Team-oriented
Devoted	Joyful	Tenacious
Diligent	Kind	Tough
Direct	Knowledgeable	Trustworthy
Disciplined	Legendary	Uninhibited
Driven	Loving	Visionary
Easygoing	Meticulous	Wealthy
Empathetic	Motivated	World-class

(Copyright © 2024 Dr. Pamela Seraphine)

Live Your Future Self in the Present

The premise of this technique is to build your future identity through intentional self-directed neuroplasticity. Unlike the "fake it till you make it" approach, where most people simply act as if they've already achieved their goals without real change happening beneath the surface, this method taps into the brain's ability to form new neural connections and rewire itself over time.

The difference is profound. The "fake it till you make it" mindset relies on external projection—pretending to be something you're not yet and hoping that over time, you'll become that person. This often leads to feelings of inauthenticity, imposter syndrome, and frustration when deep-seated change doesn't occur.

But this method goes beyond that. Neuroscience shows that by intentionally engaging in repetitive, positive behaviors and thoughts, you can reshape the neural pathways in your brain. This method isn't about projecting a false identity—it's about gradually transforming into your future self by consistently acting in alignment with the traits you want to develop. This process rewires your brain on a fundamental level, leading to real, lasting change, rather than a temporary facade.

When you ask your brain empowering questions like:
- How would a courageous, passionate, optimistic person handle this situation?
- What would they say?
- What actions would they take?

You're not pretending to be someone else. Instead, you're guiding your brain to build new neural pathways that align with the person you want to become. This process takes time, but the changes are real, grounded in neuroscience, and far more effective than the shallow, temporary results that come from faking it.

This technique is rooted in the science of self-directed neuroplasticity, which means you are actively shaping your brain to support your desired identity. This isn't about faking courage or optimism—it's about rewiring your brain so that you naturally embody those traits over time. Each small step you take reinforces new neural connections, creating lasting change from the inside out.

The key difference here is that this approach isn't about pretending or putting on a façade. It's about authentic transformation, using a scientifically-backed method to create the future self you truly desire. This process is far more effective because it aligns with how your brain actually works, rather than relying on superficial behavior alone.

This is certainly a technique that many people find difficult to implement. However, it's not because it's hard to do, but because most people believe it won't work! I challenge you to follow through with this one. Don't skip over it in pursuit of something else. It's a mandatory skill to master.

A Case Study: From Lost to Purposeful

Here's how it works in practice: A few years ago, I worked with a client who had hit rock bottom after serving time as a federal offender. Her life had been consumed by addiction and unresolved trauma, but it wasn't always that way. Before her downward spiral, she was a high performer—sharp, resourceful, and seriously resilient. But when we first started working together, her self-identity had crumbled, and she was deep in a pit of shame, grief, and regret.

During our work together, she described herself with words like "lost," "suicidal," and "depressed." I could see that while these words reflected who she was in survival mode, they definitely didn't align with who she wanted to become. Deep down, she craved a new identity defined by being "happy," "successful," and "passionate."

Now, let's be real—that's a massive leap. Moving from "lost, suicidal, and depressed" to "happy, successful, and passionate" is a hell of a stretch, especially when you're battling addiction and unresolved trauma. But here's what she discovered: she wasn't defined by the old stories her brain kept feeding her. She wasn't limited to a lifetime of seeing herself as an addict, an ex-offender, or a morally corrupt person. She was her soul, and that soul still had the capacity to cultivate traits that aligned with her future self. The first step was accepting that transformation wasn't about faking it till she made it. It was about taking small, consistent actions that aligned with the new identity she wanted to step into.

We focused on controlling what was within her grasp using the 90-Day Sprint Goals framework (more on this in the upcoming chapters). Instead of getting bogged down by comparing her life to others who seemed to have it all together, we zeroed in on what she could do each and every day—no matter how small her progress was, it still moved her closer to becoming that happy, successful, and passionate version of herself she dreamed of being. Implementing these techniques daily, even when it felt like nothing was changing, was key. Every little win counted.

Each time she embraced the behaviors and followed through with the promises she made to herself, her future identity was being created. Every action taken was another small step toward embodying the happy, passionate, and successful woman she aspired to be. She was retraining her brain to support that transformation.

Over time, those small wins added up. Her identity began to shift. The more she acted in ways that aligned with being happy, passionate, and successful, the more her brain accepted this new narrative. It didn't happen overnight, and it wasn't always smooth sailing, but that's the point—you're always becoming. The process of becoming your future self is never about pretending; it's about taking tangible steps that shift your identity from who you are now to who you're meant to be.

This is what I want you to take away: No matter where you start, you have the ability to take control of your transformation. You can choose to get your brain working for you instead of against you. But it takes daily, deliberate action. It takes the commitment to show up for yourself, even when it feels uncomfortable, even when progress seems slow. The key isn't pretending you've already arrived at your future identity—it's knowing that every step you take is bringing that future self closer to reality.

A Personal Story: Bold, Brilliant, and Beautiful

Let me share a deeply personal story about how I first began stepping into my future identity. As a child, I was subjected to intense psychological and emotional abuse from someone who should have been a source of support. Instead, this person constantly tore me down with harsh and degrading words. They repeatedly called me "fat, dumb, and ugly," embedding these toxic labels into my mind. This wasn't just occasional name-calling—it was a relentless narrative that I internalized, shaping how I saw myself throughout my formative years.

When you're a child, you're especially vulnerable to the messages you receive, and if those messages are negative, they can seep into your brain wiring and take root. Those words weren't just insults—they became a part of my identity. Even as I grew older and began to achieve more in life, the echoes of those labels lingered. Despite my accomplishments, those words still influenced how I viewed my abilities, my self-worth, and even what I believed was possible for me.

For a long time, I carried a chip on my shoulder. I was determined to prove this person and others wrong. Anger can be a powerful motivator, and in some ways, it pushed me to achieve things I might not have otherwise pursued. But here's the thing: When your motivation is rooted in anger and defiance, it only takes you so far. I wasn't truly free. I was still chained to that identity of being "fat, dumb, and ugly" because, deep down, I hadn't fully replaced those beliefs with something better.

When I began diving into the principles of applied neuroscience and self-directed neuroplasticity, I realized that I had the power to change the words that defined me. But I didn't just want to choose words that felt safe or comfortable—I wanted words that would challenge me to grow into a person I could be proud of, someone who truly embodied the greatness I was aiming for.

So, I chose three words that, at the time, felt completely out of reach: bold, brilliant, and beautiful. Just writing those words down felt like a lie. They triggered shame and discomfort because they went against everything I had been taught to believe about myself. I could feel the internal resistance—the voice that said, *Who do you think you are to call yourself bold, brilliant, and beautiful?* There was so much self-doubt and a sense that I didn't deserve to own those words.

This resistance wasn't just psychological—it was deeply ingrained in my nervous system. When you've been told repeatedly that you're less than, your brain wires itself around that belief. Even when I decided to embrace these new words, it felt like I was going against years of conditioning. But I knew that if I didn't confront this discomfort head-on, I'd stay stuck in that old identity.

So, every day, I made a deliberate choice to engage in what I call "identity embodiment." Each morning, I'd start by writing down those three words—bold, brilliant, and beautiful—in my journal. Then I'd consciously step into those words, asking myself how the bold, brilliant, and beautiful version of me would think, make decisions, and show up in the world. I made it a point to take actions that aligned with this future identity, even if it felt uncomfortable or unfamiliar.

At first, it felt awkward, even ridiculous. There were days when I wanted to throw in the towel because it seemed like I was forcing something that just didn't feel true. But here's the thing about neuroplasticity—real change doesn't happen overnight! It takes consistent repetition and a willingness to push through the discomfort until those new neural pathways are established.

Over time, as I stuck with this process, I noticed subtle shifts. I began dressing in a way that reflected boldness—I wore colors and styles that I would've never considered before. I started speaking up more, expressing my thoughts directly instead of holding back to make others comfortable. I even allowed myself to feel pride in my intellect and my accomplishments, something I used to shy away from out of fear of being judged as arrogant.

But the biggest shift happened internally. I began to feel a sense of ownership over those words. They were no longer just aspirational—they were becoming integrated into my identity. I wasn't just pretending to be bold, brilliant, and beautiful; I was becoming that person.

I'll be honest with you—it took years of dedication. Sometimes I'd choose different words to describe my identity along the way. But I'd always make my way back to the words that scared me the most. I knew this wasn't a quick fix or a motivational gimmick. It required daily practice, self-compassion, and the willingness to face my insecurities head-on. My transformation was worth every ounce of that effort. Today, I can say with confidence that I am bold, brilliant, and beautiful—not because someone else told me so, but because I put in the work to redefine my identity on my own terms.

I share this story not to boast but to show you that no matter how deeply ingrained your old identity might be, you have the power to change it. The process isn't about pretending or faking it—it's about actively rewiring your brain to align with the person you aspire to be. You have the same potential within you. By consistently embodying your chosen words and taking action that reflects those qualities, you'll gradually shift how you see yourself. And as your identity shifts, so does your reality.

Why This Approach Works

It's important to recognize that there's no one-size-fits-all solution to personal growth, brain mastery, or lasting success. Different techniques work for different people, and you have the option to test out what works best for you. Traditional models of psychotherapy, such as psychoanalysis, have helped countless individuals over the years. However, the way we understand the brain and personal transformation has evolved significantly, especially with advancements in neuroscience.

Rather than dismissing other approaches, I want to highlight how this technique (and others in this book) builds on a rich history of understanding the mind, body, and soul while integrating the latest in brain science. What sets this work apart is the practical application of self-directed neuroplasticity and a holistic view that brings together your brain, mind, body, and soul to create lasting change.

Yes, some aspects of this approach may overlap with traditional ideas in certain ways, but the key difference lies in how you actively reshape your brain. This isn't about focusing solely on past experiences or unconscious drives, as in traditional psychoanalysis. It's about empowering you to take control of your brain's wiring through intentional practices that foster growth and transformation in real-time. The tools and strategies provided here are meant to give you practical steps that you can implement daily to align your brain with your highest potential.

This method is not positioned in opposition to traditional approaches but rather as an innovative and complementary system for those seeking a dynamic, brain-based path to Neuro-Mastery. It's about offering you another tool for transformation, rooted in both the wisdom of past insights and the power of modern neuroscience.

Brain-Based Explanation: Why the Power of Three Strategy Works

This approach taps into your brain's natural capacity for change, allowing you to rewire and strengthen the neural pathways that align with your future identity. When you consistently focus on embodying specific words or traits, your brain adapts, reinforcing the connections that support those qualities. This deliberate repetition shifts your mindset and behaviors, ultimately reshaping the way you perceive yourself and the world around you.

Here's how it breaks down:

1. **Neuroplasticity in Action**: Each time you consciously choose thoughts, behaviors, and actions that align with your future identity, you're strengthening the corresponding neural pathways. Over time, these pathways become more dominant, making it easier for your brain to default to those traits naturally.[6]
2. **The Power of Repetition**: Repetition is key to retraining your brain. The more you engage in behaviors and thoughts aligned with your chosen identity words, the stronger those pathways become. Your brain is like a muscle: the more you work it in a certain direction, the more it adapts to support that direction.[7]
3. **Breaking Old Patterns**: By focusing on your future identity, you're actively disrupting the old, unhelpful patterns of thought that keep you stuck in your current identity. As you do this consistently, your brain starts to prune away those old pathways (a process known as synaptic pruning) and reinforce the new ones.[8]
4. **Emotional Integration**: Embodying a future identity isn't just about thinking differently—it's about feeling differently, in the emotional sense. When you visualize yourself as your future self, you're engaging both your cognitive and emotional systems, creating a holistic shift in how you perceive yourself.[9]
5. **Aligning with Your Core Values:** When you choose identity words that align with your core values and aspirations, you're more likely to stay motivated and committed to the process. This alignment creates a sense of authenticity, making it easier to take consistent action even when it's challenging [10]

This is how you leverage the science of neuroplasticity to create lasting change in your identity. The more you practice, the more your brain adapts, and before you know it, you'll find yourself naturally embodying the traits you once thought were out of reach.

Chapter 5 Takeaways

Don'ts:

- **Don't pretend to be someone you're not.** Focus on becoming your future self through action, not pretending you're already there.
- **Don't choose words that feel comfortable.** Growth happens when you're uncomfortable. Challenge yourself.
- **Don't get discouraged by setbacks.** You'll forget to do this sometimes—that's okay. What matters is that you keep coming back to it.
- **Don't compare yourself to others.** Everyone's starting point is different. Focus on your own progress.

Do's:

- **Do be honest with yourself.** Identify your current identity words with brutal honesty. This self-awareness is crucial for transformation.
- **Do choose words that challenge you.** Select three words that push you out of your comfort zone and align with who you want to become.
- **Do take consistent small steps.** Every time you act in alignment with your future identity, it's a win that reinforces those neural pathways.

Chapter 5 Summary: Creating Your Future Identity

In this chapter, we explored the concept of creating your future identity by tapping into the power of self-directed neuroplasticity. It's not about faking it until you make it, but rather rewiring your brain to align with the person you aspire to become.

I offered you the *Power of Three* strategy, which involves identifying three words that capture who you want to be, and using those words to guide your thoughts, actions, and behaviors. This process of embodying your future identity helps build new neural pathways that reinforce the traits you're aiming to develop.

The chapter also emphasized the importance of honesty, consistency, and commitment as you go through this transformation. You don't need to pretend you're already the person you want to be. Instead, focus on taking small, actionable steps every day that gradually move you closer to your future self.

Lastly, we dived into the science behind why this approach works, highlighting how neuroplasticity allows you to literally reshape your brain by focusing on the qualities you want to develop. By consistently practicing these techniques, you're setting yourself up for long-term growth and stepping confidently into the life you want to create. This chapter lays the foundation for intentionally crafting your future self, helping you break free from limiting beliefs and step powerfully into the greatness you're aiming for.

Myth 6: Stress is always bad for your brain.

Truth: Not all stress is harmful. Short bursts of stress can actually enhance brain performance, making you more alert and focused. The key is learning to manage stress rather than eliminating it completely (McEwen, 2007). Remember, the best time to change your brain is often in the midst of those stressful moments. You'll benefit from teaching your brain new ways to respond and showing it that you won't relinquish control unless it's to your benefit.

CHAPTER 6

Bulletproofing Your Values

*"If you avoid conflict to keep the peace,
you start a war inside yourself."*
−Cheryl Richardson

You might think you already know what your values are, but I doubt it. It's easy to fall into the trap of assuming you're clear on what matters most to you. But unless you've recently revisited them with the mindset of the adult you are now, chances are your values are still rooted in preconditioned beliefs imposed by others. That's a serious problem, and it needs a tangible solution because boundaries—or the lack thereof—are directly tied to your values. And your goals should be as well.

I learned this lesson the hard way. For a long time, I had no idea what it meant to define my values, let alone how they related to boundaries or my pursuit of greatness. I paid a massive price for that ignorance in the form of grief, loss, and betrayal of what was truly important to me. This issue is very common, especially among trauma survivors. When you've never been taught about values and boundaries—or worse, when they were never an option—you end up living life with a hazy understanding of what truly matters to you.

Even if you didn't experience childhood trauma, you might still have been navigating life without a clear sense of your values. You can drift along believing you know what you stand for, but until those values are clearly defined, they're just vague ideas with no real power. That's why this chapter is a non-negotiable read. It's going to provide you with a rock-solid strategy for defining your values and, more importantly, for bulletproofing them so you never lose sight of what matters most.

Consequences of Misalignment

Understanding and solidifying your values isn't just some feel-good exercise. It's essential for reducing stress, enhancing your overall well-being, and living a life that's aligned with your soul. Living in alignment with your core values activates brain regions associated with reward and satisfaction, like the limbic system and the prefrontal cortex. This alignment leads to a sense of purpose, fulfillment, and, ultimately, a more meaningful life.

But when your values aren't aligned with how you're living, you're in for serious consequences—emotional pain, stress, and a gradual spiraling out of control. The impact might not show up immediately, but over time, the disconnect between your values and your reality will eat away at your overall health and quality of life. If you don't bulletproof your values, you risk finding yourself lost in the abyss, disconnected from who you are and what truly matters to you.

Your values are signposts. They guide your beliefs, behaviors, and interactions with others. They form the foundation for setting goals and making decisions that bring you genuine fulfillment. So, if you're unclear on your values, it's time to change that.

Identifying Your Core Values

Before we dive into identifying your core values, let's acknowledge something important: Your brain is a master at playing tricks on you. It can convince you that you value something when you actually don't—or that you don't value something when you really do. If you're pretending to live in alignment with certain values that don't resonate with your soul, your brain will detect the misalignment and trigger a stress response. You'll end up suffering without even realizing why.

I see this all the time with my clients. They think they know what their values are, but when asked to name them, they struggle because they've never had a clear framework for identifying them. Their values are vague, wishy-washy ideas that don't provide any real guidance. I was the same way for years. How are you supposed to know what you value if you've never been taught how to figure that out?

Without clearly defined values, you end up living a life you don't want, becoming someone you never intended to be, and tolerating situations that are completely out of alignment with what truly matters to you. All because you never had the opportunity or the know-how to do this work. And your brain will rationalize it as "normal" because it's what you've always known.

But here's where you take control. I'm about to give you a simple yet effective technique for identifying and bulletproofing your core values so you can finally live in alignment with them.

Step 1: Identify Your Values

Start by taking a look at the list of values provided in this book. Your goal is to identify your top 10 core values—five that are non-negotiable and five that are secondary but still significant.

Your top five non-negotiables are the values you absolutely refuse to live without. They often remain consistent throughout your life. However, your five secondary values may change depending on your stage in life or personal circumstances. They're still important, but they're more flexible.

For example, health might not be a top priority until a serious illness forces it to the forefront. By then, it's often too late. I've had clients facing terminal illnesses or struggling with alcohol-related diseases who never valued health until their bodies began to break down. Don't wait until you're forced to re-evaluate your priorities—take control now. Carefully go through the list provided and pick your top 10 core values. Be prepared for your brain to try to trick you into thinking you value something you actually don't. That's to be expected.

Choose Your Top 10 Core Values

You must have a clear understanding of what you value most to ensure you never abandon, drop, or compromise what means the most to you. Choose your top 5 non-negotiable values and top 5 secondary values. *Identify your own.*

Acceptance	Family	Reliability
Achievement	Financial Security	Resilience
Adaptability	Forgiveness	Resourcefulness
Adventure	Freedom	Respect
Altruism	Friendship	Responsibility
Ambition	Fun	Reverence
Appreciation	Generosity	Risk-Taking
Authenticity	Gentleness	Safety
Autonomy	Grace	Security
Balance	Gratitude	Self-discipline
Beauty	Growth	Self-expression
Belonging	Harmony	Self-mastery
Boldness	Happiness	Self-respect
Challenge	Health	Sensuality
Change	Honesty	Sex
Comfort	Hope	Sharing
Commitment	Human Rights	Silence
Community	Humor	Solitude
Compassion	Humility	Spirituality
Competency	Inclusion	Sports & Fitness
Confidence	Independence	Status
Connection	Influence	Success
Contribution	Initiative	Teamwork
Control	Integrity	Time
Cooperation	Intuition	Tolerance
Courage	Job Security	Tradition
Creativity	Joy	Travel
Curiosity	Justice	Trustworthiness
Dignity	Kindness	Truth
Discipline	Knowledge	Understanding
Diversity	Leadership	Uniqueness
Education	Learning	Unity
Efficiency	Legacy	Usefulness
Enthusiasm	Logic	Vision
Equality	Love	Vulnerability
Ethics	Loyalty	Wealth
Excellence	Prestige	Well-being
Faith	Privacy	Winning
Fairness	Recognition	Wisdom
Fame	Religion	

(Copyright © 2024 Dr. Pamela Seraphine)

Step 2: Assess Alignment

Once you've identified your values, it's time to assess whether your life is actually in alignment with them. Go through each value and ask yourself: *Is my life or lifestyle aligned with this value?* Mark "NA" for not in alignment or "A" for aligned. Be brutally honest. Don't convince yourself that you're aligned when you're not.

This exercise is where most people hit a wall. They want to believe they're living in alignment, but when challenged to back it up, the truth becomes clear. It's common for people to be more aligned with their secondary values than with their non-negotiables. That's a wake-up call, and it's one that can completely change your life. You're going to need to go through them one at a time. If you are unsure, ask yourself: *What tangible proof do I have that I am living my life in alignment with this value?* Remember, you can't bullsh*t your way through this. It does you no good. Living in alignment with your core values is mandatory if you want to achieve sustainable greatness. Every decision, every goal, and even small daily choices should be made with your values in mind. When you're clear on what you stand for, you're far less likely to tolerate situations or relationships that don't serve you. And, you're far more likely to keep the promises you make to yourself.

Brain-Based Explanation: Why Bulletproofing Your Values Works

Bulletproofing your values is a brain-savvy strategy that rewires your neural pathways to reduce stress and improve decision-making. When you're clear on your values and align your actions with them, you're giving your brain a roadmap that leads to a more fulfilling, purpose-driven life. Believe me when I say, you have to keep this list out so that you can refer to it often. If you don't, a week from now you'll only remember two or three of them and your life will start going sideways again. If you find you're dealing with conflict or having to make a decision about something important, get this list in front of you and ask yourself, *Is what I'm about to do in alignment with my core values? If so, which ones?* Be specific. This is not the time for yes and no answers. Your future identity is counting on you to stay in alignment and your potential for greatness is dependent on it.

Here's how it works:

1. **Activation of Reward Pathways**: When you live in alignment with your values, your brain's reward pathways light up. The prefrontal cortex (responsible for decision-making and self-regulation) and the limbic system (which manages emotions and reward) synchronize. This creates a sense of satisfaction and reinforces positive behaviors, leading to greater well-being and resilience.[1]

2. **Reduction of Cognitive Dissonance**: When your actions conflict with your values, it creates cognitive dissonance—a state of mental discomfort that your brain detects as a threat. This misalignment increases stress and anxiety, triggering your brain's fight-or-flight response. By defining and consistently aligning with your values, you reduce this dissonance, leading to a calmer nervous system and a more focused brain.[2]

3. **Enhanced Decision-Making**: Your values act as mental shortcuts for decision-making. When faced with choices, your brain can quickly assess whether they align with your core values, allowing you to make decisions more confidently and without second-guessing yourself. This clarity reduces decision fatigue and helps you avoid choices that lead to regret or misalignment.[3]

4. **Strengthened Neural Pathways**: By regularly reassessing your values and living in alignment with them, you're engaging in self-directed neuroplasticity. Every time you make a decision based on your values, you reinforce the neural pathways associated with those principles. Over time, this makes living according to your values

second nature, reducing the mental strain of constantly questioning yourself.[4]

5. **Stress Regulation**: Living in alignment with your values activates the brain's parasympathetic nervous system—the part responsible for rest and relaxation. This reduces cortisol levels and helps regulate your stress response, allowing you to approach challenges from a place of calm and stability instead of panic and reactivity.

Real-Life Example: Values in Action

Let me share a real-life example that demonstrates how misalignment with core values can lead to profound suffering. I once worked with a highly successful entrepreneur who was devastated when his 27-year marriage ended. He had spent his entire adult life committed to raising a family, providing financial stability, and living by values like integrity, courage, and hard work. On the surface, he was doing everything "right," yet his marriage still fell apart.

When we dug deeper into his values, we discovered that he was living in alignment with four non-negotiable: values of loyalty, family, commitment, and hard work. But despite this alignment, he was suffering deeply. The real issue was that he had dismissed six of his other values because they had little to do with his spouse. They were things that were soul-fulfilling only to him, and he let them go. By the time he faced the loss of his marriage, he then started doubting whether any of his values were still worth holding onto. This is a common pitfall we all face: when someone else doesn't value what we hold dear, it's easy to start doubting whether those values are even valid.

But here's a crucial lesson: You cannot force someone to value what you do. No matter how much logic, care, or effort you put into trying to make them see the importance of your values, it won't work if they don't resonate with them. And if you start compromising what's most important to you—whether it's integrity, family, or self-respect—just to keep the peace or hold onto a relationship, you'll end up betraying yourself. It's completely your responsibility to live in alignment with what matters most to you. This doesn't mean your spouse or partner has to have the same ones as you do, but they at least have to be compatible. For example, if you have loyalty as a non-negotiable and your partner doesn't have it in any of their top 10, there is going to be trouble coming down the pipeline. Don't ever assume someone has the same values as you do. Don't even assume they know what they are. They most likely don't.

Living in alignment with your core values is about taking ownership of your life and choices. It's about trusting that when you stay true to what matters most, the right people and opportunities will naturally align with you. This applies whether you're a man, a woman, or anyone who wants to live a life free from regret. Your values are yours to uphold, and when you honor them, you build a foundation that's unshakeable, no matter who comes and goes in your life.

Personal Story: Blind Spots and Hard Lessons

As I mentioned earlier, there was a time when I had no clue what my values were, let alone how to bulletproof them. I thought I knew what I valued, but I was clueless about how deeply my beliefs were shaping my life. For the longest time, I focused on health, family, and self-expression. As a musician and a mother, those seemed like the obvious priorities.

But here's what I didn't realize: There were other values I deeply cared about—like contribution, autonomy, and wealth—that I wasn't even aware of because they were buried under outdated beliefs. For example, I had internalized the belief that money was the root of all evil, so I never made wealth a priority. I believed that if I mastered my craft, the money would follow. That limiting belief kept me broke for most of my adult life. It wasn't until I consciously decided to value wealth that things began to change. Once I made that value a priority, I started taking actions that aligned with it. And guess what? My financial situation improved dramatically. It was a blind spot that seriously cost me until I faced it head-on.

As I worked to realign my values, I also began to notice a shift in the types of relationships I attracted. When I prioritized what truly mattered to me—like contribution, autonomy, and even wealth—I naturally started drawing in people who shared those values. This included friendships, professional connections, and now I'm even open to the possibility of finding a soulmate who resonates with my newly aligned life.

Knowing what your values are puts you in a position of power. It allows you to attract what you want in your life, and what you will and will not tolerate. This is why identifying and bulletproofing your values is so crucial. You have to confront your blind spots and take control of what matters most to you. If you don't, you'll suffer the consequences—whether that's losing relationships, missing out on opportunities, or simply living a life that feels unfulfilling. But when you align with your deepest values, you unlock the freedom, purpose, and clarity needed to create a life that truly reflects your highest potential. The choice is yours. Own your values, and watch everything else, including the right relationships, fall into place.

Chapter 6 Takeaways

Don'ts:

- **Don't ignore misalignment.** The price you'll pay for living out of alignment with your values is high. Don't let it slide.
- **Don't let others impose their values on you.** If someone values something that doesn't resonate with you, it's not you. It's them. Your values are yours alone.
- **Don't overlook the consequences.** Ignoring your values leads to long-term emotional pain and suffering. Take this seriously—your brain and your soul depend on it.

Do's:
- **Do seek clarity.** Take the time to clearly define your top 10 core values. Knowing what you stand for will guide your decisions and behaviors.
- **Do be honest with yourself.** Be truthful about what truly matters to you. Challenge your brain if you start questioning whether something is of real value.
- **Do reassess regularly.** Check-in with your values approximately every 90 days to ensure your goals and lifestyle are still aligned with what matters most.

Chapter 6 Summary: Bulletproofing Your Values

In this chapter, we tackled a key pillar of personal greatness: defining, clarifying, and bulletproofing your core values. It's easy to think you know your values, but many people unknowingly follow beliefs imposed by others, leading to stress, dissatisfaction, and misalignment. I covered the cost of living out of sync with your values—cognitive dissonance, heightened stress, and a lack of purpose.

I also outlined how to identify your top 10 core values—five non-negotiables and five secondary ones—by getting brutally honest with yourself. But knowing your values isn't enough; it's mandatory to regularly assess if your life truly aligns with them. This involves evaluating whether your actions and choices consistently reflect your core principles. Finally, we examined the brain science behind bulletproofing your values. Aligning your behavior with your values strengthens positive neural pathways, reduces cognitive dissonance, and rewires your brain for sustained success and fulfillment.

Myth 7: Happiness is the ultimate goal.

Truth: Chasing happiness as the ultimate goal can lead to dissatisfaction. Neuroscientific studies show that pursuing purpose and meaning, rather than fleeting happiness, creates deeper fulfillment and rewires the brain for long-term well-being (Steger et al., 2008). This is one of the most detrimental myths out there. If you chase happiness as a core value, you will suffer the consequences. However, your values are yours to define.

CHAPTER 7

Slaying Your Goals

"There will always be the 1 percent of us who are willing to put in the work to defy the odds."
–David Goggins

Achieving your goals and realizing your dreams can feel like a beast of a journey. The process of choosing, setting, and accomplishing goals is full of unlimited obstacles. Many people either quit or end up compromising their well-being and soul in the pursuit. Even with self-discipline and knowledge of every goal-setting strategy out there, the path can still be overwhelming and confusing. So don't be surprised if, in the past, you've either failed to reach your goals or achieved them at a high personal cost. There is a good reason for this.

The primary reason goal-setting and goal achievement are so tough is that conventional methods often clash with how your brain is naturally wired.[1] Plus, staying aligned with *your soul's* desires is a massive challenge—and one that's easy to dismiss until it's too late. In this chapter, I'm going to introduce you to a method that merges brain science with soul care. The 90-Day Sprint Goal Framework is a brain-based, soul-aligned strategy designed to help you achieve extraordinary success without sacrificing your well-being.

The Backstory: From Survival to Success

As I mentioned in the introduction, it took me well over a decade—starting in my mid-30s—to go from a high school dropout, single mom of three, living in poverty, to earning a doctorate degree with honors. That's a long haul to stay committed to your dreams, especially when the odds are stacked against you. For someone like me—who spent most of her life in survival mode—achieving that goal was monumental.

But here's the truth: While I did achieve my goal, I did it at a tremendous personal cost. For years, I relied on sheer mental toughness, discipline, and work ethic. I read all the books, understood the SMART goal framework, and knew how to push through adversity. But I didn't have a system that protected my sanity or preserved my soul. I had no idea how to balance achievement with the pressures, loneliness, and heartbreak that came with grinding toward my dreams.

It wasn't until I immersed myself in sports psychology, neuropsychology, and the neurobiology of trauma that I started to realize I was missing critical skills. Personal development rarely addresses the complex emotional and psychological challenges that arise when you're striving for greatness. The "grind" might get you results, but it'll wear you down if you don't have a framework that nurtures both your brain and soul. That's where the 90-Day Sprint Goal Framework comes in. It's designed to help you flourish in both your personal and professional life without sacrificing one for the other.

Your Brain and Goals: How It Really Works

From a brain-based perspective, well-defined goals act like magnets. When they're clearly thought out, documented, and aligned with your values, they compel your brain to focus and move toward the target.[2] Specific goals give your brain a tangible reason to overcome obstacles and align with your soul's desire for a compelling future. Without this alignment, you'll likely achieve your goals sporadically and in an unhealthy, unsustainable way.

You don't need a PhD in neuroscience to slay your goals, but you do need to understand how to prevent your brain from sabotaging your efforts. Protecting yourself from psychological injury and emotional pain while striving for greatness is crucial. Personal greatness—lasting success paired with deep fulfillment—becomes achievable when your brain and soul work in harmony.

Red Flag Warning Signs

Before diving into the 90-Day Sprint Goal Framework, be aware of two primary red flags that could derail your progress: negative self-talk and limiting beliefs. These subtle yet powerful obstacles can have a significant impact if not addressed.

Red Flag Warning #1: Negative Self-Talk

Your brain is naturally wired to focus on the negative as a survival mechanism.[3] This negativity bias often shows up as self-sabotaging thoughts like *I'll never be able to do this,* or *Why does this always happen to me?* Such thoughts are reinforced by neurochemistry, arising from past experiences, failures, or critical feedback that your brain has internalized and replays on a loop. While it might sound strange, this negative self-talk is your brain's misguided attempt to protect you from perceived threats or disappointments.[4]

As you embark on your 90-Day Sprint, watch out for these three common self-sabotaging patterns:

- **Fear of Inadequacy:** Thoughts like *I'm not smart enough* or *I'll never be able to handle this* can paralyze you before you even begin, leading you to doubt your abilities and avoid taking action.
- **Fear of Failure:** Worries like *What if I succeed and can't handle it?* or *What if I fail and people laugh at me?* will keep you stuck in a cycle of inaction, making you hesitant to take risks or pursue new opportunities.

- **Perfectionism**: Perfectionistic thoughts like *If it's not perfect, it's not worth doing* can trap you in endless cycles of overthinking, preventing you from making progress or finishing what you start.

The C.A.R. Technique: Countering Negative Self-Talk

Combat these patterns with the C.A.R. technique:
1. **Conscious Awareness:** First, recognize when you're engaging in negative self-talk. Awareness is the critical first step toward change.
2. **Ask the Question:** Challenge the thought by asking, *Is this thought moving me closer to or further away from what I want?* This reframes the situation, allowing you to see the thought for what it is—a barrier, not a truth.
3. **Replace with "Who:"** Shift your focus by asking, *Who can help me achieve this?* This question engages your brain's problem-solving abilities and activates neurochemicals like oxytocin (for connection) and dopamine (for motivation), which can help you push forward with renewed energy and confidence.[5]

Brain-Based Explanation: Why the C.A.R. Technique Works

The C.A.R. technique leverages principles from cognitive neuroscience and behavioral psychology to counteract negative self-talk and reframe disempowering thoughts. Here's why it's effective:
1. **Conscious Awareness (C):** Your brain processes thousands of thoughts each day, many of which run on autopilot. Negative self-talk often slips by unnoticed, but conscious awareness interrupts this automatic cycle. By actively recognizing these thoughts, you engage the prefrontal cortex and remember that it's the brain region responsible for executive function, decision-making, and self-regulation. This shift from unconscious to conscious processing gives you control over your thoughts, rather than letting them control you.[6]

2. **Ask the Question (A):** Asking whether a thought is moving you closer to or further away from your goals introduces cognitive dissonance when the answer is negative. This dissonance signals your brain that the current thought is not aligned with your desired outcomes, triggering a need for change. The brain seeks consistency, so this dissonance motivates it to adopt more adaptive thoughts that support goal achievement.[7]

3. **Replace with "Who" (R):** Replacing the negative thought with an empowering "who" question—like *Who can help me achieve this?*—shifts your focus from problems to solutions. From a neurobiological standpoint, this taps into the brain's problem-solving circuitry, involving regions like the dorsolateral prefrontal cortex. Additionally, engaging in social thinking and collaboration activates the brain's reward pathways, releasing oxytocin (for connection) and dopamine (for motivation), creating a positive feedback loop that reinforces goal-oriented behaviors.[8, 9]

Red Flag Warning #2: Limiting Beliefs

Limiting beliefs are deeper, more ingrained convictions that silently hold you back. These beliefs often stem from your brain's interpretation of past experiences, societal conditioning, or unresolved trauma. Left unchecked, they can quietly undermine your progress and sabotage your efforts.

Here are some common limiting beliefs to watch out for:

- **Unworthiness:** Thoughts like *I don't deserve to be happy,* or *What's wrong with me?* These beliefs fuel constant self-sabotage by convincing you that you're unworthy of success or fulfillment, even when you've worked hard to achieve them.

- **Fixed Mindset:** Beliefs like *I've always been this way,* or *It's impossible to change* create mental barriers that stop you from embracing challenges or learning from failures, limiting your growth and potential. Embrace the Outlier Mindset.

- **Perceived Lack of Control**: Statements like *I've tried everything, and nothing works,* or *Success is all about luck* reflect a victim mindset that strips you of agency and limits your motivation to pursue your goals.

The A.C.T. Technique: Overcoming Limiting Beliefs

To overcome these limiting beliefs, apply the A.C.T. technique:

1. **Awareness:** Start by consciously identifying the belief. For example, say, *I believe [limiting belief]*. Naming it gives you power over it.
2. **Challenge the Belief:** Ask yourself, *Is this belief based on facts or feelings?* Look for evidence that contradicts the belief. Often, you'll find that the belief is rooted in feelings rather than objective reality.
3. **Transform:** Shift your mindset by creating an empowering "why" question. For example, instead of saying, *I'll never be able to achieve this goal,* ask, *Why is it possible for me to achieve this goal?* This approach engages your brain's problem-solving capabilities and focuses your attention on solutions rather than limitations.

Brain-Based Explanation: Why the A.C.T. Technique Works

The A.C.T. technique (Awareness, Challenge, Transform) is rooted in cognitive restructuring, a method proven to alter deep-seated limiting beliefs. Here's how it works from a neuroscience perspective:

1. **Awareness (A):** Identifying and stating your limiting beliefs brings them from the subconscious to the conscious mind. The brain's reticular activating system (RAS) filters information that aligns with these beliefs, making it easy for them to remain hidden. By consciously bringing them into awareness, you disrupt this filter and open the door for reprogramming.[11]
2. **Challenge the Belief (C):** Challenging whether a belief is based on facts or feelings activates critical thinking processes in the prefrontal cortex. By analyzing the belief logically, you weaken the emotional

grip it has on you. This step also taps into neuroplasticity by creating new pathways as you reframe your thinking. When you start questioning long-held beliefs, your brain begins to prune away the old, limiting pathways (through synaptic pruning) and replace them with more adaptive and growth-oriented ones.[12]

3. **Transform (T):** Transforming the belief into an empowering "why" question reorients your brain toward positive possibilities. "Why" questions are inherently open-ended, prompting your brain to search for evidence and solutions. This engages your brain's default mode network (DMN), which is responsible for introspection and future planning. As your brain finds answers that support your new belief, it reinforces these pathways, making them stronger and more dominant over time.[13]

The 90-Day Sprint Goal Framework

Now, let's dive into the action plan. The 90-Day Sprint Goal Framework is designed to help you achieve more in 90 days than most people do in an entire year. It's all about harnessing your brain's natural tendencies while staying in alignment with your soul's desires. You can download a free PDF printout of this framework using the QR code at the end of the chapter. You'll also have access to a supporting video that I created to help you better understand your 90-Day Sprint!

The framework consists of five elements:
1. **Start Date and End Date:** Mark the start and end dates for your 90-Day Sprint. This timeframe is specifically chosen: It's long enough to retrain neural pathways and short enough to maintain focus and momentum.
2. **Future Identity Words:** Choose three words that describe the person you want to become—someone who could achieve the goals you're setting. We covered this topic in Chapter 5.

3. **Core Values:** Your goals must align with your top 10 core values. If they don't, they're not worth pursuing. We covered this topic in Chapter 6.
4. **Primary Goal and Two Secondary Goals:** Your primary goal should be a stretch, but achievable within 90 days. It should align with your core values and push you beyond your comfort zone. It requires that you sprint towards it to achieve it within your timeframe! Your secondary goals should be challenging but easier to achieve, offering balance and maintaining motivation. Having one primary goal is all about singularity of focus. You've got to train your brain to laser in on the actions that bring you closer to that goal—nothing else matters. If it's not pushing you forward,cut it out. Sure, your secondary goals have value, but they shouldn't demand nearly the energy or time that your primary goal does. Your main goal needs to be the one that creates the biggest shift in your life—the kind that makes you jump out of bed every morning, fired up and ready to crush it. It should light such a fire within you that you don't have time to waste on anything less important. Hence, the reason it needs to be aligned with your values.
5. **Signature:** Commit to your goals with integrity by signing your name at the bottom. This is your contract with yourself.

The hardest part of this challenge is staying relentlessly committed to your goals. Your brain is wired to sabotage you, serving up every excuse in the book—and even convincing you that you don't really want that goal anymore. When that happens, you've got to tell your brain to "f*ck all the way off" and stay laser-focused on what you truly want. Don't let your own brain stand in the way of your greatness.

Dr. Pamela Seraphine
NEUROSCIENTIST | TRAUMA EXPERT | MUSICIAN

90-DAY SPRINT GOALS ACTION PLAN

To optimize your 90-day sprint, you must prioritize the goals that mean the most to you and are aligned with your values. Your goals should be well-defined, measurable, and just beyond your comfort zone.

START DATE: _____ **END DATE:** _____

3 WORDS TO DESCRIBE YOUR FUTURE IDENTITY:

1. _____ 2. _____ 3. _____

TOP 10 VALUES

1. _____
2. _____
3. _____
4. _____
5. _____
6. _____
7. _____
8. _____
9. _____
10. _____

PRIMARY GOAL
This is your #1 priority goal. It should have the biggest impact on your life in the shortest amount of time possible.

I am fully commited to achieving my goal of
_____

My reward for this accomplishment is
_____

SECONDARY GOAL
I am fully commited to achieving my goal of
_____

My reward for this accomplishment is
_____

SECONDARY GOAL
I am fully commited to achieving my goal of
_____

My reward for this accomplishment is
_____

(Copyright © 2024 Dr. Pamela Seraphine)

Frequently Asked Questions: Crushing Your 90-Day Sprint with Clarity and Confidence

When it comes to executing a 90-Day Sprint, having a clear strategy is crucial. But even with the best plans, questions and doubts are guaranteed to creep in along the way. That's where this FAQ section comes in. I've compiled the most important questions to ensure you stay focused, maintain momentum, and avoid common pitfalls. Whether you're wondering how to choose the right goal, stay motivated, or manage setbacks, these answers will give you the clarity and confidence to crush your sprint—and elevate every aspect of your life in the process.

Remember, mastering this sprint is about more than just hitting a target. It's about becoming the version of yourself who is unstoppable, resourceful, and laser-focused. You got this!

1. **How do I choose the right primary goal for my 90-Day Sprint?**

    Answer: Your primary goal should stretch you, but still be achievable within 90 days. It must align with your core values and push you beyond your current limits. Start by asking yourself:

    –What one goal, if achieved, would have the most significant positive impact on my life?
    –What are the benefits I'd experience from achieving this goal?
    –What would it cost me if I didn't achieve it?
    –Is this goal aligned with my core values and the future identity I'm committed to?

    Make sure your goal resonates deeply with your future identity and the person you're becoming. And once you commit, keep the promises you make to yourself—no matter what.

2. **Can I set more than one goal for my 90-Day Sprint?**

    Answer: While your focus should be on one primary goal, you can set one or two secondary goals. These don't need to be related to your primary goal, but they can add balance and variety, keeping you engaged and preventing burnout. Just remember, your primary goal is the one that should light a fire under you every single day.

Staying committed is the real challenge here! Your brain will throw every excuse at you, convincing you these goals don't matter anymore. Don't let it win.

3. **What should I do if I don't achieve my 90-Day Sprint Goal?**

   Answer: Not hitting your goal doesn't mean you've failed. The 90-Day Sprint is about stretching your limits and forcing growth. If you come up short, take it as a learning opportunity. Reflect on what held you back, and roll your unfinished goals into the next sprint. The key is to reassess, realign, and refocus. Never give up—keep pushing until you hit your target.

4. **How can I stay motivated throughout the 90-Day Sprint?**

   Answer: Staying motivated is non-negotiable, and it starts with aligning your goals with your core values and future identity. Track your progress regularly using a results tracker (coming up in Chapter 9), celebrate small wins, and always stay connected to your "why." The B.O.S.S. Method in Chapter 8 will help keep your intentions, focus, and identity sharp every day.

5. **How do I ensure my 90-Day Sprint Goals align with my long-term vision?**

   Answer: Your 90-Day Sprint Goals should be stepping stones toward your long-term vision. But remember, after every 90 days, you should be a completely new and improved version of yourself. Your thoughts, actions, identity, and even your desires will evolve.

   I highly recommend creating a yearly plan with only three priorities—each from different areas of your life, like Family, Career, and Health. Start by defining your yearly goals, then break them into

90-day sprints. Each sprint should get you closer to your ultimate objectives while keeping you focused on immediate, achievable milestones.

At the end of your 90-Day Sprint, if you're not slightly embarrassed by who you were 90 days ago, you didn't push yourself hard enough!

6. **What if I encounter unexpected obstacles during my 90-Day Sprint?**

   Answer: Obstacles are part of the game. When they show up, use the C.A.R. Technique to keep your mindset in check—Conscious Awareness, Ask the Question, and Replace with "Who." Reframe challenges as opportunities to grow and adapt. If necessary, tweak your strategies, but never abandon your goals. Flexibility is key to maintaining momentum.

7. **How do I maintain balance between my 90-Day Sprint Goals and other life responsibilities?**

   Answer: I'm not a fan of the word "balance" in this context. It's unrealistic when you're chasing something extraordinary. You're going to swing between extremes. Some areas of your life might need to be put on pause for a while. That's why every 90 days, you've got to re-evaluate and see if your priorities have shifted.

   What I'm teaching you is about creating harmony, not balance. It's a holistic approach to personal greatness. Just like elite athletes use periodization for peak performance, you'll prioritize high-impact activities aligned with your 90-Day Sprint Goals while still keeping an eye on your overall well-being. Use the results tracker (coming in Chapter 9) to monitor both your progress and your well-being—soul care, relationships, and personal growth included.

8. **How do I manage setbacks or plateaus during my 90-Day Sprint?**

   Answer: Setbacks and plateaus are inevitable, but they're also signals for growth. When you hit a wall, it's time to assess what's not working and adjust your approach. Start by identifying the bottlenecks—are they mental, emotional, or strategic? Then, reframe the situation: What is this challenge teaching you, and how can you use it to level up? Remember, the difference between success and failure lies in how quickly you adapt and course-correct. Don't get stuck; instead, lean into discomfort and use it as fuel to push through to the next level.

9. **What role does accountability play in the 90-Day Sprint, and how can I incorporate it?**

   Answer: Accountability is a game-changer. Share your goals with a trusted friend, mentor, or even work with me as your 1-on-1 coach to keep you on track. You can also join a group of like-minded individuals pursuing their own 90-Day Sprints through my coaching program, Neuro-Mastery: 12 Weeks to Unlock Your Personal Greatness. Regular check-ins and updates provide that extra layer of support and motivation, ensuring you stay the course when challenges arise.

10. **How can I ensure my soul controls my brain during the 90-Day Sprint?**

    Answer: Your soul and brain must work in unison for true alignment. You need a resilient soul to keep your brain in check. Throughout the 90-Day Sprint, soul care is non-negotiable. Make sure you're fueling it with activities that bring you joy and excitement—even if they aren't directly related to your goals. Never underestimate the power of an empowered soul! Both top-down and bottom-up techniques are essential during your sprint. Surround yourself with positive influences that align with your goals and identity. And remember, training your brain daily allows it to face anything with both grit and grace. When your soul leads, your brain follows with unwavering focus.

Brain-Based Explanation: Why the 90-Day Sprint Goal Framework Works

The 90-Day Sprint Goal Framework is based on principles of neuroplasticity, motivation science, and behavioral conditioning. Here's why it's so effective:

1. **Optimizing Timeframes for Sustainable Change**: The 90-day period is a sweet spot for creating new habits and neural pathways. Research shows that it takes approximately 67 days to establish a new habit, but a 90-Day Sprint allows for both habit formation and reinforcement. During this time, your brain undergoes significant synaptic changes, strengthening the connections that support your goals. By committing to a 90-day period, you leverage neuroplasticity to create lasting change.[14]

2. **Alignment with Core Values and Future Identity**: Goals that are aligned with your core values and future identity engage the brain's limbic system (responsible for emotion and motivation) and the prefrontal cortex (responsible for planning and decision-making). When your goals resonate with your deeper sense of purpose, your brain perceives them as more rewarding, increasing dopamine (molecule of desire) release. This neurochemical boost enhances focus, motivation, and the likelihood of following through.[15]

3. **Leveraging the Brain's Reward System**: The 90-Day Sprint Goal Framework creates a structured approach to achieving short-term wins, which are critical for maintaining momentum. Each time you hit a milestone, your brain releases dopamine, reinforcing the behavior and creating a positive feedback loop. The more consistently you experience these rewards, the more motivated you become to stay committed, making the framework highly effective for sustained goal achievement.[16]

4. **Overcoming the Brain's Resistance to Change:** The brain naturally resists change because it perceives uncertainty as a threat. The 90-Day Sprint Goal Framework introduces manageable, time-bound challenges that are just outside your comfort zone. This approach balances the need for growth with the brain's preference for predictability, allowing you to stretch without overwhelming your system. By gradually building up tolerance to discomfort, you reduce the brain's tendency to self-sabotage and create a path for consistent progress.[17]

Final Thoughts

The 90-Day Sprint Goal Framework is more than just a goal-setting strategy—it's a life transformation system that aligns your actions with your deepest values and future identity. Remember, you don't get to change your mind halfway through. Once you commit, you're all in. By sticking to this framework, you'll cultivate the discipline, adaptability, productivity, and focus needed to unlock your personal greatness. I'm going to give you a case study of how this all ties together later in the book. Keep moving forward!

Chapter 7 Takeaways

Don'ts:

- **Don't Set Random Goals.** Avoid setting goals that aren't aligned with your core values or future identity. Random goals lack purpose and will leave you feeling disconnected and unfulfilled.
- **Don't Ignore Negative Self-Talk.** Failing to address negative self-talk will sabotage your efforts and create unnecessary stress and doubt. Confront it head-on using proven strategies.
- **Don't Cling to Limiting Beliefs.** Don't allow outdated or fear-based beliefs to control your decisions. Challenge them, transform them, and choose empowering thoughts that support your growth.

- **Don't Isolate Yourself.** Trying to achieve your goals alone can lead to burnout and a reduction in motivation. Seek support, collaborate with others, and tap into resources that help you stay on course.
- **Don't Shy Away from Challenges.** Growth happens when you face discomfort and challenge yourself. Don't avoid difficulties—embrace them as a vital part of your path toward personal greatness.

Do's:

- **Do Define Clear, Measurable Goals:** Set goals that are specific, actionable, and just beyond your comfort zone. They should be challenging enough to push you to grow but achievable within the 90-day framework.
- **Do Align Your Goals with Core Values.** Your goals should resonate deeply with at least a couple of your top 10 core values. This alignment ensures that every step you take is purposeful and that the results will bring you genuine fulfillment.
- **Do Stay Aware of Red Flag Warning Signs.** Recognize and address negative self-talk and limiting beliefs as soon as they arise. These mental traps are your brain's attempt to protect you, but they can also hold you back from greatness.
- **Do Use the C.A.R. and A.C.T. Techniques.** Implement the C.A.R. (Conscious Awareness, Ask the Question, Replace with "Who") and A.C.T. (Awareness, Challenge the Belief, Transform) techniques to counter self-sabotage and keep your mindset on track.
- **Do Commit Fully to Your 90-Day Sprint Goals.** When you set a goal, stick to it for the entire 90 days. Your brain will try to convince you to quit, but staying committed is where real growth and transformation happen.

Chapter 7 Summary: Slaying Your Goals

Slaying your goals doesn't have to come at the cost of your well-being. In this chapter, I introduced you to the 90-Day Sprint Goal Framework, a brain-based strategy that aligns your goals with your core values and future identity. This approach empowers you to achieve extraordinary success without compromising your mental, emotional, physical health and spiritual health.

The framework leverages your brain's natural tendencies, allowing you to focus with laser precision on what matters most. By incorporating your core values, future identity, and actionable goals, you create a powerful roadmap that guides you toward success while keeping your soul's desires front and center.

The key is to stay vigilant against red flags like negative self-talk and limiting beliefs. These mental barriers are designed to protect you but often hold you back from reaching your true potential. With tools like the C.A.R. and A.C.T. techniques, you can override these obstacles and maintain momentum, even when the going gets tough.

Remember, achieving your goals is about more than just crossing items off a list—it's about becoming the person who can achieve those goals while thriving in every area of life. The 90-Day Sprint Goal Framework gives you a blueprint for doing just that. By committing fully to your goals and embracing the process, you can create lasting change, achieve remarkable results, and experience the fulfillment that comes from living a life aligned with your highest values.

Your goals aren't just dreams—they're the roadmap to your future identity. When you combine your brain's capabilities with your soul's deepest desires, you become unstoppable. The next chapters will dive deeper into refining this process, offering even more insights and strategies to ensure your journey toward personal greatness is both successful and sustainable.

Myth 8: Multitasking makes you more productive.

Truth: Your brain isn't wired to multitask. In reality, switching between tasks reduces focus and efficiency. The brain performs best when it's locked into a single task with full attention (Ophir et al., 2009). It's easy to believe you're incapable of deep-focused work, especially if you've been diagnosed with ADHD. But once again, challenge that limiting belief! Your brain is capable of learning how to focus and concentrate for extended periods of time. It just takes conscious effort and self-discipline. It may be difficult, but the rewards far outweigh the effort. Don't let your brain tell you otherwise.

CHAPTER 8

Becoming the B.O.S.S.

*"Winning f*cks with your mind. It just does."*
−Tim Grover

I can't emphasize enough how important it is to become the BOSS of your brain. This is no joke. As I mentioned in the introduction, your brain is powerful enough to sabotage any chance you have of creating the life you want and deserve—if you let it. You can't just allow it to do whatever it wants. That's a recipe for pain, suffering, and an unfulfilled life. You can't start your day without considering how your brain affects your thoughts, behaviors, and worldview, especially if you're serious about achieving greatness and crushing those seemingly impossible goals.

Your brain is hardwired to prioritize survival at all costs, often in the most dysfunctional ways possible.[1] If you're not in control, it will run wild, derailing your progress and keeping you trapped in old patterns. That's why it's absolutely essential to take command of your brain from the moment you wake up until the moment you go to sleep. You must consciously stay in control of your brain to keep it aligned with your goals.

Do you remember the G.L.A.D. technique I introduced in Chapter 2? That was a small step in taking conscious control of your brain, particularly as a nighttime practice. Now, I'm giving you the ultimate morning routine—the B.O.S.S. Method—designed to supercharge your day and align every action with your 90-Day Sprint Goals. This method isn't easy to stay committed to. It's an elite strategy for those ready to elevate their Neuro-Mastery to a whole new level. That's you. Right?

The B.O.S.S. Method: The Ultimate Morning Routine

B.O.S.S. is an acronym that stands for: Become Aware, Offer Intention, Suggest Focus, and Secure Identity. By mastering this method, you'll not only take control of your brain but set a powerful tone for your entire day. The B.O.S.S. Method is intricately connected to your 90-Day Sprint Goals and is designed to bring you closer to personal greatness.

Let's break down each step.

Step 1: Become Aware—Take Command of Your Brain

From a brain-based perspective, awareness is the foundation for all change. By becoming aware and taking command of your brain first thing in the morning, you activate your prefrontal cortex (the thinking brain), which enhances planning, decision-making, and goal pursuit. The moment you open your eyes, start by observing your mental and emotional state without judgment, then take control by speaking directly to your brain.[2]

Remember, your brain is a separate entity from your soul, and it needs direction. Craft a morning mantra that resonates with you—something that signals your conscious awareness and reminds your brain that you're in charge. Here are a few examples:
- I'm in charge today; you'll do as I say.
- Good morning, brain. Let's crush this day.
- F*ck off, brain. I'm running the show today.

This practice not only builds the neural pathways supporting resilience and mental clarity but also sets the tone for your entire day. Your soul (your conscious self) needs to check in with your brain constantly, ensuring that you remain in control. Creating a morning mantra signals that you're taking the lead and that your brain's default patterns won't dictate your actions.

Step 2: Offer Intention—Set the Tone for Your Day

Setting a clear intention primes your brain's reticular activating system (RAS), which filters information and focuses your attention on what aligns with your goals. By offering your intention directly to your brain, you guide it to recognize opportunities and direct your actions in alignment with your 90-Day Sprint Goals.[3]

Every morning, articulate and write down a specific intention that aligns with your values and desired outcomes. Examples include:

- "My intention is to work for 45 minutes with full commitment and enthusiasm."
- "My intention is to have a joyful, stress-free day."
- "My intention is to complete three focused hours on my primary goal with integrity and excellence."

By starting with intention, you set the stage for a purpose-driven day that's in alignment with your core values.

Step 3: Suggest Focus—Direct Your Brain's Full Power

Getting your brain to focus on the tasks you assign is crucial to productivity and goal achievement. By suggesting a focal point for your day, you engage your prefrontal cortex's executive functions, helping prioritize tasks and manage attention.

Choose one or two primary focuses for the day, directing your brain's energy to where it's needed most. Examples include:

- Focus on finding new strategies to support my primary goal.
- Focus on connecting with someone who can help me reach my 90-Day Sprint Goal.
- Focus on cultivating more joy in alignment with my value for happiness.

You're telling your brain what to focus on, keeping it aligned with what matters most. This step is key to staying on track and cutting through the noise of distractions.

Step 4: Secure Identity—Reinforce Your Future Self

The final step involves reinforcing your identity by repeating your future identity words daily. Securing your identity through affirmation strengthens the neural pathways linked to your self-concept and primes your brain to take actions aligned with your goals.[4]

Examples include:
- I am becoming a courageous, focused, and disciplined leader.
- I am becoming a creative, resilient, and powerful entrepreneur.
- I am becoming a calm, confident, and self-assured professional.

Remember, these aren't empty statements. They're declarations rooted in who you're becoming through your actions and commitments. The more consistently you repeat this practice, the more aligned your thoughts and behaviors become with your desired identity. Be sure to use the statement "I am becoming," until your actions clearly support "I am" statements.

Real-Life Example: Overcoming Sabotage in My Strength Zone

Let me share a personal story that shows how the B.O.S.S. Method and 90-Day Sprint Goals play out in real life. One of my most challenging yet meaningful goals was creating the "Mastering Peak Performance for First Responders" masterclass. On the surface, this goal was squarely in my strength zone—I had the expertise, the experience, and a proven track record in this area. The goal aligned perfectly with my core values of social contribution, growth, and excellence. I was confident that this was work that mattered and that I was uniquely positioned to deliver.

Yet, even in familiar territory, resistance crept in.

It's a common misconception that when you're working within your strength zone, you're immune to self-doubt or fear of failure. The truth is, the closer you get to something that matters, the louder your brain's protective mechanisms scream at you. My brain, even with all its knowledge and experience, kept throwing up barriers—doubts like, *No one in the first responder community is going to care about this!* Or, *You're trying to reach a culture that doesn't trust outsiders!* It was relentless in its attempts to sabotage my progress.

But I was prepared for this. I knew what my brain was doing, and I had the B.O.S.S. Method in place to counter it. Here's how I stayed in control:

- **My morning mantra:** I'm in charge today; you'll do as I say.
- **My intention:** Today, my intention is to complete Module 2 with integrity and excellence, staying laser-focused on transforming lives.
- **My focus:** Brain, focus on finding inspiration and creative solutions to keep this project aligned with my values.
- **My identity:** I am a passionate, influential, and innovative leader.

With each step, I made sure my soul was steering the ship—not my brain's fear-driven programming. Every time self-doubt reared its head, I reminded my brain who's really in charge. The B.O.S.S. Method became my daily go-to, allowing me to push through resistance and stay true to my values and mission.

The result? I not only completed the masterclass but delivered something truly impactful. The feedback I received validated the immense effort and intention behind the work it took to create. Knowing I had overcome my own brain's attempts to derail this goal made the achievement even more meaningful. It's this kind of control—where your soul commands your brain—that keeps you aligned with your higher purpose and drives you toward greatness.

Case Study: Reclaiming Power and Self-Respect through Rhythmic Mastery

Here's an example of how the B.O.S.S. method and the 90-Day Sprint Framework played out for my client. A few years ago, I worked with a 56-year-old military veteran, I'll call him Steve. He had survived more chaos and trauma than most people are able to imagine. Steve was a man who had faced hell and walked through fire, yet here he was, battling deep depression, buried resentment, and stuck in a soul-crushing, abusive relationship. He was tough as nails on the outside—years of military conditioning made sure of that—but inside, he was hanging on by a thread.

His wife was verbally and emotionally abusive, constantly tearing him down. The psychological torment was relentless. Like many mentally tough men, he suffered in silence. He'd been conditioned to endure, to push through, to never let anyone see his truth. But beneath the surface, the constant barrage of emotional abuse had left deep scars. The respect he once held for himself had eroded, and it was painfully clear that he was no longer living in alignment with the values that had once been his guiding light—values like honor, respect, and integrity.

When he came to me, he was desperate to get his life back on track. He had no job, felt utterly disconnected from himself, and was drowning in anger and bitterness. We began by digging deep into his values, and it was no surprise that his self-respect was in shambles. One of his top non-negotiable values was respect, yet he wasn't showing any to himself. He'd become so focused on treating others with respect that he had completely forgotten that respect had to start with him. This was his blind spot—the glaring contradiction that was keeping him stuck in a cycle of suffering.

Together, we designed his 90-Day Sprint Goals, with the primary focus on rebuilding his self-respect. But here's the thing about self-respect: It isn't given. It's earned. You can't just decide one day that you respect yourself. You have to prove it through action by keeping the promises you make to yourself, even when it's hard.

Steve's primary goal was to secure stable employment, a step toward regaining his sense of dignity and financial independence. His secondary goals were to hit the gym three times a week, strengthening his body and reinforcing his commitment to his health, and to master six rhythmic mantras—a deceptively challenging goal that would test his discipline, focus, and mental fortitude.

Let's talk about these rhythmic mantras because they are a beast of a challenge. This is part of the NRTT Method I mentioned earlier. These aren't just simple drumming patterns; they are intricate, meditative sequences designed to push the limits of mental discipline. Each level of mantras consists of complex rhythms that require intense focus, self-control, and a deep connection to the process. For Steve, these mantras were more than just exercises—they were a battle. Each time he sat down to practice, he was faced with the urge to quit, to give in to that voice in his head telling him it was pointless, that no one would care whether he succeeded or failed.

But that's exactly why these mantras mattered. Every time Steve chose to stay committed, every time he pushed through the frustration and finished a practice session, he was reclaiming a piece of his self-respect. The rhythmic mantras became a mirror of his internal struggle—they reflected his ability to overcome the chaos in his mind and find a sense of calm amidst it.

Steve's 90-Day Sprint Goals were difficult and meaningful to him. He wrestled with self-doubt, battled his brain's attempts to sabotage him, and faced the harsh reality that earning back his self-respect was going to be an uphill climb. But day by day, using the B.O.S.S. Method, he took control of his brain and stayed the course. His morning mantra was direct and raw, reflecting his military background: *Get your shit together, brain. F*ck off and do as I say.* His intentions were laser-focused: *My intention is to stay disciplined, stay calm, and not let anyone—including myself—derail my progress.* His focus was relentless: *Focus on mastering this damn mantra. Every* *beat matters*. And his identity words—self-disciplined, calm, and happy—began to take root as he lived them out in real-time.

By the end of the 90 days, Steve had not only secured a job, but had also begun to get his physical health back on track and mastered those six mantras. This was a remarkable feat! But more importantly, he earned back something that had been lost for years—his self-respect. The abusive relationship didn't magically end, and his life wasn't suddenly perfect. But he was different. He had rebuilt a foundation of self-worth that no one could take away from him. He had proven to himself that he could keep his promises, no matter how tough the road got.

Steve's story is a powerful reminder that self-respect isn't just about setting boundaries with others—it's about setting boundaries with yourself and honoring them. It's about proving to yourself, day in and day out, that you have what it takes to live in alignment with your values, no matter what life throws at you. That's what it means to become the B.O.S.S. of your brain, and that's what it takes to truly master your life.

Chapter 8 Takeaways:

Don'ts:

- **Don't Let Your Brain Run on Autopilot.** Avoid starting your day without consciously directing it to do what you want it to do. Your brain is wired for survival, not success.
- **Don't Neglect Your Values.** Don't overlook the importance of staying aligned with your core values. You'll pay a price for it if you do.
- **Don't Shy Away from Challenges.** Growth requires discomfort. Avoiding difficult tasks that push you outside your comfort zone will only keep you stuck.
- **Don't Let Your Brain Sabotage You.** Don't allow negative self-talk or fear-based thinking to derail your progress.

- **Don't Isolate Yourself.** Avoid trying to achieve your goals in isolation. Seek support and collaboration when needed. Connection can provide valuable resources and extra motivation.
- **Don't Underestimate the Power of Consistency.** Consistency is key to building new neural pathways and achieving sustainable change. Skipping your morning routine puts your progress at risk.

Do's:

- **Do Take Command of Your Brain.** Use a morning mantra that resonates with you to set the tone for your day.
- **Do Set Clear Intentions.** Start each day by articulating a specific intention that aligns with your values and goals.
- **Do Direct Your Brain's Focus.** Choose one or two key priorities for the day and tell your brain what to focus on.
- **Do Reinforce Your Identity Words.** Affirm your future identity words daily to strengthen your self-concept and align your actions with your goals.
- **Do Stay Consistent.** Repeat the B.O.S.S. Method every morning to maintain control and keep your brain on track.
- **Track Your Growth.** Keep a journal to monitor your progress and reflect on how you're evolving over time.

Chapter 8 Summary: The B.O.S.S. Method

In this chapter, I introduced you to the B.O.S.S. Method, a morning routine designed to help you take command of your brain and set the tone for a day aligned with your 90-Day Sprint Goals. The four steps—Become Aware, Offer Intention, Suggest Focus, and Secure Identity—ensure that you remain in control of your brain from the moment you wake up.

By following this routine, you can stay focused on what matters most, counter your brain's natural tendencies to sabotage you, and reinforce the identity you're working toward. The real-life examples I shared illustrate how this method works in both familiar and challenging situations, showing you that even when resistance and doubt creep in, you have the tools to overcome them.

Becoming the B.O.S.S. of your brain isn't just about achieving goals—it's about aligning your actions with your core values, staying true to your purpose, and living in a way that brings both success and fulfillment. The B.O.S.S. Method is your blueprint for taking conscious control of your life and becoming the person you're meant to be.

Myth 9: A perfect morning routine guarantees success.

Truth: While morning routines can set a positive tone for the day, the idea that there's a "perfect" routine that guarantees success is misleading. What works for one person may not work for another. Scientific research shows that personalizing your morning routine to align with your unique brain chemistry, energy levels, and lifestyle is far more effective for long-term success (Vallacher et al., 2012). The key is consistency, not perfection. Tailor it to your own needs and experiment with what works best for you. That said, the BOSS method is a powerful morning routine, and I encourage you to try it!

CHAPTER 9

Dominating Your Results Tracker

"To exist is to change; to change is to mature;
to mature is to go on creating one's self endlessly."
–Henri Bergson

It's easy to fall into the trap of believing that tracking your progress and celebrating your wins is unnecessary. You might think it's just extra effort that doesn't really contribute to achieving your goals. I get it, but once again, I call bullsh*t! If you believe it's not worth the effort, that's your brain messing with you. It's yet another way it tries to protect you from the fear of failure and the unknown.

But here's another truth: If you want to achieve more, you need to track your progress. The research and statistics are undeniable. Consistency in goal-setting is directly linked to two key factors: accountability and positive reinforcement. Studies show that people who write down their goals and track their progress are significantly more likely to achieve them.[1] Keeping a record of your wins holds you accountable and keeps your brain focused on your path toward success.[2] And let's not forget the power of positive reinforcement: Tracking daily wins boosts motivation, morale, and keeps you engaged. It's easy to convince yourself that small wins don't matter, but that's just your brain downplaying what's crucial to your success.

In this chapter, I'm going to share with you my proven system for tracking progress and celebrating wins. This system will ensure you dominate your results tracker and crush your goals. Tracking isn't just a motivational tool—it's a powerful way to harness your brain's natural tendencies for growth.

Why Tracking Your Wins Is Non-Negotiable: The Brain-Based Perspective

Before I move on to the strategy itself, I want to highlight why this process is non-negotiable. From a neuroscientific standpoint, tracking your wins is a game-changer. Let me break down why:

1. **Dopamine Release:** Each time you log a win, no matter how small, your brain releases dopamine—the molecule of desire. This creates a positive feedback loop, making you want to continue working toward your goals. It's not just about feeling good; it's about training your brain to crave the process of winning.[3]

2. **Neural Pathway Reinforcement:** Consistently tracking your progress helps reinforce the neural pathways associated with success and achievement. The more you repeat these behaviors, the easier it becomes for your brain to engage in productive actions. Your brain and soul both know when you're keeping or breaking promises to yourself.[4]

3. **Cognitive Load Reduction:** Writing down your goals and tracking your progress reduces the cognitive load on your brain. This frees up mental resources for problem-solving and creative thinking. You can't afford to let your brain get bogged down in clutter—it needs clarity to operate at peak performance state.[5]

4. **Enhanced Self-Regulation:** Regular tracking strengthens your prefrontal cortex—the thinking part of your brain responsible for decision-making, self-control, and goal-oriented behavior. The

more you practice self-regulation, the better you become at staying on course, even when distractions or temptations arise.[6]

To make this process foolproof, I created the 90-Day Results Tracker as the ultimate tool for tracking daily wins. The primary reason I designed it was that many of my clients made significant progress but were unaware of just how far they'd come. They'd complete a 90-Day Sprint, undergo major transformations, yet have no clue how they got there. They'd look back and think their growth was a small miracle, forgetting all the effort it took to achieve it. From a brain-based perspective, this is disempowering and counterproductive. Overlooking your daily wins means you're missing out on crucial positive reinforcement needed to sustain long-term growth. If you don't experience daily wins, your brain will revolt and revert to old, dysfunctional behaviors. That's the last thing you want.

Implementing the 90-Day Results Tracker

The 90-Day Results Tracker involves six categories that are essential for your path toward personal greatness. Each day, you'll ask yourself a series of questions and mark an X next to each win you achieve. By doing this, you'll stay aware of your progress holistically and reinforce the positive behaviors and mindset shifts that align with your 90-Day Sprint Goals.

Here's a breakdown of each category:

1. **Insight Win:** *Ask yourself, Did I experience an "aha" moment or a paradigm shift today?* From a brain-based perspective, experiencing these insights means your brain is making new connections and expanding your understanding. Recognizing these moments reinforces the neural pathways supporting innovative thinking and problem-solving. Every time you consciously note an insight, you're proving that you're evolving beyond autopilot and becoming more mindful. That's personal greatness.[7,8]

2. **Behavior Win:** Ask, *Did I take action toward any of my 90-Day Sprint Goals today?* Taking action activates your brain's reward system, releasing dopamine and reinforcing positive behaviors. Marking each action solidifies productive habits and keeps your brain engaged. If you exceed expectations, your brain releases more dopamine, pushing you further. Celebrate every action, no matter how small—it's a win.[9,10]

3. **Soul Care Win:** Ask, *Did I do something to bring more joy into my life today?* Joyful activities stimulate the release of endorphins and serotonin, enhancing mood and overall well-being. Soul care is about nurturing your emotional and mental health, which directly impacts productivity and fulfillment. I've found that soul care is often the most challenging for people because they undervalue its importance. But it's non-negotiable. This is about building a formidable soul that can override the inner workings of your brain.[11,12]

4. **Boundary Win:** Ask, *Did I assert healthy boundaries today?* Setting boundaries engages the prefrontal cortex, enhancing self-regulation and decision-making. Boundaries protect your mental space and energy, allowing you to focus on what truly matters. While I didn't dive deep into boundary-setting earlier in this book, it's critical because it's tied directly to your values. If your values are compromised, your brain will constantly perceive threats, leading to chronic stress and burnout.[13,14]

5. **Top-Down Win:** Ask, *Did I use my mind to retrain my brain today?* Top-down strategies, like cognitive-behavioral techniques and mindfulness, are essential for lasting positive change. Each time you intentionally use your mind to shift your thoughts, you're rewiring your brain toward resilience and growth.[15,16]

6. **Bottom-Up Win:** Ask, *Did I use my body to retrain my brain today?* Bottom-up techniques, such as physical exercise, deep breathing,

and rhythmic entrainment (like drumming), directly impact your brain's emotional and stress regulation centers. These practices reset your nervous system and create a stable foundation for mental and emotional health.[17,18,19,20,21]

90-DAY SPRINT RESULTS TRACKER

*Ask yourself the following questions **every day** and mark an "X" to support your wins!*

1. **Insight Win:** Did I experience an "aha" moment or paradigm shift?
2. **Behaviour Win:** Did I take action toward any of my 90-day sprint goals?
3. **Soul-Care Win:** Did I do something to bring more joy into my life?
4. **Boundary Win:** Did I assert healthy boundaries?
5. **Top-Down Win:** Did I use my mind to retrain my brain?
6. **Bottom-Up Win:** Did I use my body to retrain my brain?

Start Date:

End Date:

WEEK 1
	S	M	T	W	T	F	S
INSIGHT WIN:	○	○	○	○	○	○	○
BEHAVIOUR WIN:	○	○	○	○	○	○	○
SOUL-CARE WIN:	○	○	○	○	○	○	○
BOUNDARY WIN:	○	○	○	○	○	○	○
TOP-DOWN WIN:	○	○	○	○	○	○	○
BOTTOM-UP WIN:	○	○	○	○	○	○	○

WEEK 2
	S	M	T	W	T	F	S
INSIGHT WIN:	○	○	○	○	○	○	○
BEHAVIOUR WIN:	○	○	○	○	○	○	○
SOUL-CARE WIN:	○	○	○	○	○	○	○
BOUNDARY WIN:	○	○	○	○	○	○	○
TOP-DOWN WIN:	○	○	○	○	○	○	○
BOTTOM-UP WIN:	○	○	○	○	○	○	○

WEEK 3
	S	M	T	W	T	F	S
INSIGHT WIN:	○	○	○	○	○	○	○
BEHAVIOUR WIN:	○	○	○	○	○	○	○
SOUL-CARE WIN:	○	○	○	○	○	○	○
BOUNDARY WIN:	○	○	○	○	○	○	○
TOP-DOWN WIN:	○	○	○	○	○	○	○
BOTTOM-UP WIN:	○	○	○	○	○	○	○

WEEK 4
	S	M	T	W	T	F	S
INSIGHT WIN:	○	○	○	○	○	○	○
BEHAVIOUR WIN:	○	○	○	○	○	○	○
SOUL-CARE WIN:	○	○	○	○	○	○	○
BOUNDARY WIN:	○	○	○	○	○	○	○
TOP-DOWN WIN:	○	○	○	○	○	○	○
BOTTOM-UP WIN:	○	○	○	○	○	○	○

WEEK 5
	S	M	T	W	T	F	S
INSIGHT WIN:	○	○	○	○	○	○	○
BEHAVIOUR WIN:	○	○	○	○	○	○	○
SOUL-CARE WIN:	○	○	○	○	○	○	○
BOUNDARY WIN:	○	○	○	○	○	○	○
TOP-DOWN WIN:	○	○	○	○	○	○	○
BOTTOM-UP WIN:	○	○	○	○	○	○	○

WEEK 6
	S	M	T	W	T	F	S
INSIGHT WIN:	○	○	○	○	○	○	○
BEHAVIOUR WIN:	○	○	○	○	○	○	○
SOUL-CARE WIN:	○	○	○	○	○	○	○
BOUNDARY WIN:	○	○	○	○	○	○	○
TOP-DOWN WIN:	○	○	○	○	○	○	○
BOTTOM-UP WIN:	○	○	○	○	○	○	○

WEEK 7
	S	M	T	W	T	F	S
INSIGHT WIN:	○	○	○	○	○	○	○
BEHAVIOUR WIN:	○	○	○	○	○	○	○
SOUL-CARE WIN:	○	○	○	○	○	○	○
BOUNDARY WIN:	○	○	○	○	○	○	○
TOP-DOWN WIN:	○	○	○	○	○	○	○
BOTTOM-UP WIN:	○	○	○	○	○	○	○

WEEK 8
	S	M	T	W	T	F	S
INSIGHT WIN:	○	○	○	○	○	○	○
BEHAVIOUR WIN:	○	○	○	○	○	○	○
SOUL-CARE WIN:	○	○	○	○	○	○	○
BOUNDARY WIN:	○	○	○	○	○	○	○
TOP-DOWN WIN:	○	○	○	○	○	○	○
BOTTOM-UP WIN:	○	○	○	○	○	○	○

WEEK 9
	S	M	T	W	T	F	S
INSIGHT WIN:	○	○	○	○	○	○	○
BEHAVIOUR WIN:	○	○	○	○	○	○	○
SOUL-CARE WIN:	○	○	○	○	○	○	○
BOUNDARY WIN:	○	○	○	○	○	○	○
TOP-DOWN WIN:	○	○	○	○	○	○	○
BOTTOM-UP WIN:	○	○	○	○	○	○	○

WEEK 10
	S	M	T	W	T	F	S
INSIGHT WIN:	○	○	○	○	○	○	○
BEHAVIOUR WIN:	○	○	○	○	○	○	○
SOUL-CARE WIN:	○	○	○	○	○	○	○
BOUNDARY WIN:	○	○	○	○	○	○	○
TOP-DOWN WIN:	○	○	○	○	○	○	○
BOTTOM-UP WIN:	○	○	○	○	○	○	○

WEEK 11
	S	M	T	W	T	F	S
INSIGHT WIN:	○	○	○	○	○	○	○
BEHAVIOUR WIN:	○	○	○	○	○	○	○
SOUL-CARE WIN:	○	○	○	○	○	○	○
BOUNDARY WIN:	○	○	○	○	○	○	○
TOP-DOWN WIN:	○	○	○	○	○	○	○
BOTTOM-UP WIN:	○	○	○	○	○	○	○

WEEK 12
	S	M	T	W	T	F	S
INSIGHT WIN:	○	○	○	○	○	○	○
BEHAVIOUR WIN:	○	○	○	○	○	○	○
SOUL-CARE WIN:	○	○	○	○	○	○	○
BOUNDARY WIN:	○	○	○	○	○	○	○
TOP-DOWN WIN:	○	○	○	○	○	○	○
BOTTOM-UP WIN:	○	○	○	○	○	○	○

Developed by Dr. Pamela Seraphine

The Power of Holistic Progress

It's easy to get hyper-focused on a single goal and let other areas of your life fall apart. That's a dangerous trap that leads to inner suffering and turmoil. The price you pay for neglecting holistic progress is too high. The 90-Day Results Tracker ensures you maintain balance by keeping every aspect of your growth in check.

The real reward isn't just in achieving your goals—it's in falling in love with the process of winning each day. It's you against you, your brain against your soul. And if you miss a win, don't worry—you always have the next day to get back on track. If you're struggling to realign, it's because your brain is winning. That's when you need to reconnect with your soul and get back in control.

Unlocking Clarity: The Certainty List

There's one more hurdle that many people face: They don't know what they truly want. It's more common than you'd think, regardless of financial status, success, or power. Most people have no clear idea of what they want in their future, and that's because their brains are actively protecting them from the uncertainty that comes with pursuing big goals.

Your brain hates uncertainty.[22] It would rather keep your desires vague and out of reach than risk the failure that could come from trying to achieve them. But there's a way to force your brain to reveal what you truly want: the Certainty List.

The Certainty List is a mindful technique designed to tap into your brain's need for clarity. It involves writing down 10 things you're absolutely certain you want in your future. By focusing on certainty, you engage the prefrontal cortex and reinforce neural pathways associated with clarity, intention, and positive goal orientation.[23]

Here's how it works:

Write down 10 statements that start with "I'm certain that I want…" For example:

- I'm certain that I want to earn 100K more per year working only four days a week.
- I'm certain that I want to build a lasting, loving relationship with someone who shares my values.
- I'm certain that I want to quit my job and start my own business.

In the beginning, your answers may be vague, like "I'm certain I want to be happy," or "I'm certain I want more money." But as you practice, your brain will become more precise. The more specific and detailed your answers become, the clearer your path forward will be.

If unresolved trauma makes this exercise difficult for you, ease into it by focusing on what you're certain about in the present, like "I'm certain the sky is blue." Over time, your brain won't pick this strategy up as a perceived threat, and it will allow you to dig deeper and reveal what you truly want in your future.

Aligning Your Goals: The Key to Personal Greatness

I know I'm on repeat here, but aligning your goals with your core values, future identity words, and being certain about what you want in your future is far more than just creating a framework—you're anchoring yourself in a deep sense of purpose. This alignment is where intention meets action, where your desires are translated into a plan that not only guides you on your path but keeps you connected to the essence of who you are and who you're becoming.

When you craft goals that resonate with your core values, you ignite a fire within your soul—a fire that burns so bright it lights the path forward, even on your darkest days.

This isn't just about ticking boxes or meeting deadlines. It's about creating a life where every step you take feels right, where your pursuit of success is deeply intertwined with your sense of fulfillment and meaning. Your future identity words serve as the compass, constantly reminding you of the person you are evolving into. They hold you accountable to your highest potential, challenging you to act in ways that are congruent with that version of yourself—stronger, wiser, and more aligned than ever before.

Your Certainty List brings clarity to the equation. It forces you to cut through the noise and zero in on what truly matters. The more specific and intentional you become about what you want, the easier it is to say "no" to distractions and "yes" to the things that propel you toward greatness. This alignment is what separates those who merely dream from those who achieve. When your goals, values, identity, and soul desires are in sync, you create a life where success isn't just a possibility—it's inevitable.

But let me be clear: This kind of alignment isn't easy to achieve. It requires brutal honesty, relentless commitment, and the willingness to confront your deepest fears and desires. It's about stripping away the superficial layers and digging deep into what your soul truly craves. When you do this, you're no longer just setting goals—you're designing a life that's authentic, purposeful, and unapologetically yours.

With this alignment, your 90-Day Sprint Goals become more than just milestones. They become sacred promises to yourself, backed by the unshakeable belief that you're capable of achieving whatever you set your mind to. As you dominate your results tracker, you'll witness the transformation that happens when you live in full alignment with your values, identity, and purpose. This is how you achieve greatness—by designing a life where every action you take is a reflection of the person you're becoming, a life where your goals are not just achieved but are deeply meaningful and soul-fulfilling.

Chapter 9 Takeaways

Don'ts:

- **Don't Let Your Brain Run on Autopilot.** You can't afford to let your brain dictate your actions without conscious input. Take charge every day by directing your focus and energy toward what truly matters.
- **Don't Ignore Your Daily Wins.** Overlooking your daily wins is like missing out on the fuel that keeps your momentum going. Celebrate them—no matter how small they seem—because they're proof you're making progress.
- **Don't Avoid Challenging Goals.** If your goals aren't challenging you, they're not changing you. Embrace discomfort—it's a sign that you're growing and pushing beyond what's comfortable.
- **Don't Neglect Your Values.** Misaligned goals lead to burnout, dissatisfaction, and, ultimately, failure. Your values are your compass: Ignore them, and you'll lose your way.
- **Don't Isolate Yourself.** Going it alone is a recipe for burnout and stagnation. Connect with others who can support and uplift you. Success is sweeter when shared.

Do's:

- **Do Track Your Progress Daily.** Tracking keeps you accountable and provides the clarity you need to stay on course. The more consistent you are, the stronger your habits become.
- **Do Celebrate Your Small Wins.** Small wins aren't insignificant; they're the stepping stones to major breakthroughs. Acknowledge them: They're the fuel your brain needs to stay motivated and engaged.

- **Do Align Your Goals with Your Core Values.** Before you set a goal, check if it aligns with your core values. Goals that resonate with your values are more fulfilling and keep you motivated long-term.
- **Do Use Your Certainty List.** The Certainty List is your brain's blueprint for what you truly want. Use it to gain clarity, refine your goals, and stay focused on what's most important to you.
- **Do Seek Support When Needed:** No one achieves greatness alone. Surround yourself with people who challenge, support, and inspire you to be your best. Collaboration accelerates growth.

Chapter 9 Summary: Dominating Your Results Tracker

In this chapter, we dived into the essential practice of dominating your results tracker by consistently tracking your daily wins. This isn't just about accountability—it's about reinforcing the positive behaviors and harnessing your brain capacity to align with your 90-Day Sprint Goals. By tracking across six categories—insight, behavior, soul care, boundary, top-down, and bottom-up wins—you create a holistic approach that ensures no aspect of your growth is left behind.

I also introduced the Certainty List—a powerful tool to clarify what you truly want. This technique cuts through the brain's resistance and provides a clear roadmap for your desires, aligning them with your core values and future identity words. When these elements are in sync, your goals become more than just targets. They become extensions of who you are and who you're becoming.

This chapter equips you with the framework to ensure that every step you take is intentional, aligned, and purpose-driven. By embracing these strategies, you're not just setting yourself up for success, you're building a life where every action, every decision, and every goal is infused with meaning, fulfillment, and greatness.

Remember, your path to greatness isn't just about achieving goals—it's about becoming the person who can achieve them while staying true to your soul's desires. As you move forward, keep tracking, aligning, and pushing yourself to dominate every aspect of your path toward Neuro-Mastery. True transformation happens through the process itself. Armed with the brain-based tools you now possess, you're not just ready—you're unstoppable!

Myth 10: You can think your way out of stress.

Truth: While mindset matters, stress management involves engaging the body and regulating physiological responses (Porges, 2007). You can't simply think your way out of stress without addressing how your body processes it. Stress is not just a mental event; it affects your entire nervous system. To manage stress, you must incorporate techniques like breathwork, physical movement, and body-based strategies to calm these physiological reactions. Only then can you reset your system and regain control of your brain.

Book Recommendation: For a more comprehensive (but dense) exploration of how the Polyvagal Theory applies to stress and emotional regulation, check out Porges, S. W. (2011). The Polyvagal Theory: Neurophysiological Foundations of Emotions, Attachment, Communication, and Self-regulation. W. W. Norton & Company.

CHAPTER 10

Firing on All Cylinders

"Greatness is not an act, it's a habit. What you consistently do will determine your level of success."
–Ben Newman

You've come this far—so don't you dare let up now. There's one final challenge: integrating everything you've learned and starting to fire on all cylinders—consistently! This is where you truly separate yourself from the mediocre, the halfway committed, and the people who never quite get out of their own way.

I'm not here to sugarcoat it: Cultivating personal greatness and lasting success is hard f*cking work. Staying aligned with your core values, mastering your brain, and taking command of your future every single day is not easy—it's a relentless process. But a life filled with pain and suffering is worse. I don't need to tell you that; deep down, you already know this. That's why you picked up this book in the first place. You're here because you're not looking for quick fixes. You're here to own your life and shape it into something extraordinary.

Recognizing Your Progress

Take a moment to acknowledge how far you've come. Finishing this book means you're not interested in being average. You have much higher standards for yourself! You've progressed from understanding how your brain can sabotage you, to developing brain-based tools to counter that sabotage, to mastering the art of setting goals that align with your soul. You've learned to integrate brain-based strategies and soul care into your daily life—ensuring that your progress is not just fast but sustainable.

Throughout this book, you've explored your core values, crafted your future identity, and learned what it takes to dominate your 90-Day Sprint Goals. I've dissected the reasons behind why your brain tries to play it safe, and you've confronted the reality that achieving greatness isn't about taking shortcuts—it's about commanding every aspect of your life with intention and discipline.

But don't get comfortable. Just because you've read this book doesn't mean you can afford to coast on your progress. The moment you get comfortable, your brain will find a way to sneak back into old habits. Comfort is the enemy of growth.

The Unapologetic Truth About Mastery

Here's what nobody tells you: The moment you think you've got it all figured out is the moment you're most vulnerable. Mastery is a moving target—it evolves as you evolve. That's why this process never ends. The more you achieve, the more you have to fight against complacency, self-sabotage, and the urge to take your foot off the gas.

Firing on all cylinders isn't just about maintaining your momentum—it's about amplifying it. You've built a foundation, and now you have the opportunity to expand beyond anything you once thought possible. That's how you become someone who doesn't just succeed in spurts but consistently dominates life.

You're not here to be ordinary. You're here to become unstoppable. And to do that, you need to keep refining the strategies you've learned throughout this book. You must make your B.O.S.S. routine non-negotiable. Dominate your Results Tracker like it's your lifeline. And above all, stay committed to aligning your goals with your core values, your future identity, and the soul-deep desires that push you to be better every single day.

The good news is you don't have to do this alone. If you want to take your growth to the next level and ensure you're equipped to handle life's darkest challenges, here are some options to consider:

- **Neuro-Mastery Coaching or The NRTT Method Coaching:** These 12-week programs are designed for individuals committed to achieving excellence and pushing past their limits. Working directly with me, you'll receive personalized guidance to ensure you're firing on all cylinders in every area of your life.
- **The Hope After Trauma Academy:** More than just a collection of courses, this is a community and resource built on the same brain-based principles you've learned in this book. It's designed to help people who value peak performance and lasting transformation—especially those working in high-stress industries. Whether you're a first responder, mental health professional, or someone ready to rebuild your life stronger than ever, this is where you'll find the tools and support to make that happen.
- **Speaking Engagements and Training Sessions:** For organizations looking to elevate their teams, I offer sessions focused on corporate leadership, trauma recovery, and high-performance strategies. My unique blend of neuroscience, music, and soul care is designed to inspire and empower your team. Let's create lasting change together!

Securing Your Legacy

As you close this chapter, ask yourself: What's next? How do you continue to fire on all cylinders long after this book is done? This journey isn't just about achieving your goals—it's about securing your legacy. It's about leaving a mark on the world that's undeniable. Your brain will try to convince you that you've done enough, that you've arrived. But that's a lie. The path towards Neuro-Mastery doesn't end; it evolves. The real power lies not in reaching the finish line but in dominating every step of the race.

So, what will you do now that you know how much you're truly capable of? Will you settle for being another voice in the crowd, or will you rise above, relentless in your pursuit of personal greatness? The choice is yours. But if you've made it this far, I already know what kind of decision you'll make.

Chapter 10 Takeaways

Don'ts:

- **Don't get comfortable.** Complacency is the enemy. The second you start to coast, your brain will pull you back into old habits.
- **Don't underestimate the power of consistency.** Mastery isn't about a single breakthrough—it's about doing the work day in and day out, even when it feels tedious.
- **Don't isolate yourself.** You're only as strong as the support you surround yourself with. Seek out communities that challenge and inspire you.

Do's:

- **Do stay vigilant.** Keep refining your B.O.S.S. routine, 90-Day Sprint Goals and tracking your progress—it's what will keep you aligned and on track, especially when life throws chaos your way.
- **Do push past what's comfortable.** Growth doesn't happen in comfort zones. Keep seeking out challenges that force you to evolve.
- **Do secure your legacy.** Your goals are about more than just hitting targets—they're about leaving a lasting impact. Make every action count toward something bigger than yourself.

Chapter 10 Summary: Relentless Pursuit of Mastery

You've armed yourself with the brain-based tools, strategies, and paradigm shifts necessary to achieve your version of greatness. But this isn't the end—it's just the beginning. Firing on all cylinders means staying committed to your growth, pushing past your limits, and refusing to settle for mediocrity. Whether you continue your path toward Neuro-Mastery on your own, want one-on-one guidance from me, or dive into resources like the Hope After Trauma Academy, know that the power to dominate your life is fully within your control.

Your brain is brilliant—both in its capacity to sabotage you and in its potential to propel you to heights you never imagined. But the deciding factor has always been, and will always be, your soul. When your soul is in charge, and your brain is aligned with your deepest values and identity, you're capable of things most people wouldn't even dare to dream of.

Let me leave you with something personal. You'll remember from the introduction that I suffered a life-altering injury that ripped me out of the music industry and forced me into academia. It felt like the end of a dream I had been chasing my entire life. But I didn't let that be the final chapter. Years later, I recalibrated my drumming skills, changed my style, and now I'm playing better than ever before! I didn't just get back to where I was—I surpassed it. I achieved my goal of becoming a world-class percussionist, despite the odds.

This isn't just about mental toughness; it's about lasting success. I'm living proof that even when life knocks you down, your brain and soul have the capacity to come back stronger, more focused, and more aligned with your purpose. It's about taking control of your brain, building a formidable soul, and never letting go of what truly matters. Your challenges can become the catalyst for your greatest achievements. This is your life. Own it, dominate it, and never stop firing on all cylinders in your pursuit of personal greatness, and lasting success.

Myth 11: You can talk your way out of trauma.

Truth: While discussing trauma can be a helpful part of the healing process, lasting recovery requires addressing the body's physiological responses. Research has shown that trauma deeply impacts the nervous system and is often stored in the body, leading to chronic stress patterns (Kolacz et al., 2018). Don't be fooled into thinking otherwise. To fully recover, the brain and body must be retrained through somatic and brain-based techniques, not just talk therapy. Without addressing these physiological elements, trauma recovery remains incomplete.

Furthermore, trauma recovery doesn't have to be boring or feel like a never-ending struggle. Who has time for that?! You can create sustainable, positive change through positive experiences. The recovery process itself can be transformative, exciting, and rewarding. Ultimately, the choice is yours.

Acknowledgments

First and foremost, I want to express my gratitude to all my incredible clients who have shaped my work. It has been an honor to be a part of your journey through life. I also want to acknowledge the neuroscientists and scholars who have profoundly influenced my approach to the science of personal greatness. Special thanks to Dr. Bessel van der Kolk, Dr. Michael Taut, Dr. Daniel Levitin, Dr. Daniel Siegel, Dr. Joseph LeDoux, and Dr. Jennifer Sweeton.

I extend my sincere appreciation to Mathew Dahlitz, co-founder of The Science of Psychotherapy. Thank you for providing years of inspiration and for the kindness you showed in writing the foreword for this book. My heartfelt thanks also go to Danny Seraphine for your unwavering support over the years, even when it wasn't always clear what I was striving to achieve. My gratitude also goes to Cris Cawley and the Game Changer Publishing team for holding my feet to the fire and ensuring that this book became my ultimate sprint goal.

I want to give special thanks to Bruce Kirk and the BC Borstal Association. I'm deeply grateful for everything you've done to make my contribution to society possible. Together, our vision of what's possible is truly limitless.

To my mother, Lynn Branson, and Gregory Pederson—your unwavering love and support have meant the world to me through every challenge and triumph. I couldn't have come this far without you both. To my brother, Shawn Fostvelt—thank you for being my hype-master and for your countless questions about my work.

And finally, a special heartfelt thank you to my daughters, Jessica, Tia, and Mikia—I hope this book inspires you to achieve your own version of personal greatness, however you choose to define it.

About the Author

Dr. Pamela Seraphine is a trailblazing expert in applied neuroscience, specializing in high performance, trauma recovery, and brain-based approaches for success and fulfillment. With a unique blend of scientific expertise and creative artistry, Dr. Seraphine is also an accomplished world percussionist who integrates her artistic talents with cutting-edge research to offer a truly holistic approach to personal growth and peak performance.

As the developer of the Hope After Trauma Academy, owned by the BC Borstal Association, Dr. Seraphine has dedicated her career to empowering first responders, military personnel, and high achievers with the tools they need to excel in high-stress environments while maintaining their mental health and well-being. Her unique, brain-centric strategies are sought after by individuals and organizations alike for their proven effectiveness.

Dr. Seraphine's teachings reflect her commitment to unlocking human potential through brain mastery, offering a blend of science, soul care, and strategic tough love. She has transformed countless lives through one-on-one coaching and dynamic training programs, all while remaining a thought leader at the intersection of neuroscience, personal development, and trauma recovery.

In addition to her academic achievements, Dr. Seraphine is known for her unapologetically raw and authentic voice. Her work continues to inspire those driven to achieve greatness and live extraordinary lives—on their own terms.

THANK YOU FOR READING MY BOOK!

DOWNLOAD YOUR FREE GIFTS

Just to say thanks for buying and reading my book, I would like to give you a few free bonus gifts, no strings attached!

I appreciate your interest in my book and value your feedback as it helps me improve future versions. I would appreciate it if you could leave your invaluable review on Amazon.com with your feedback. Thank you!

Endnotes

Chapter 1: The Truth About Your Brain

1. Poldrack, R. A., & Wagner, A. D. (2004). What can neuroimaging tell us about the mind? Insights from prefrontal cortex. *Current Directions in Psychological Science, 13*(5), 177-181. https://doi.org/10.1111/j.0963-7214.2004.00299.x
2. McEwen, B. S., & Morrison, J. H. (2013). The brain on stress: Vulnerability and plasticity of the prefrontal cortex over the life course. *Neuron, 79*(1), 16-29. https://doi.org/10.1016/j.neuron.2013.06.028
3. Bremner, J. D. (2006). Traumatic stress: Effects on the brain. *Dialogues in Clinical Neuroscience, 8*(4), 445-461. https://doi.org/10.31887/dcns.2006.8.4/jbremner
4. Stanley, I. H., Hom, M. A., Hagan, C. R., & Joiner, T. E. (2019). A systematic review of suicidal thoughts and behaviors among police officers, firefighters, EMTs, and paramedics. *Clinical Psychology Review, 74,* 101809. https://doi.org/10.1016/j.cpr.2019.101809
5. World Health Organization (2021). Suicide worldwide in 2019: Global health estimates. World Health Organization. https://www.who.int/publications/i/item/9789240026643
6. Arnsten, A. F. T. (2009). Stress signaling pathways that impair prefrontal cortex structure and function. *Nature Reviews Neuroscience, 10*(6), 410-422.
7. Purves, D., Cabeza, R., Huettel, S. A., et al. (2018). *Principles of Cognitive Neuroscience* (2nd ed.). Sinauer Associates.
8. Kahneman, D. (2011). *Thinking, Fast and Slow.* Farrar, Straus and Giroux.

9. Merzenich, M. M. (2013). *Soft-Wired: How the New Science of Brain Plasticity Can Change Your Life.* Parnassus Publishing.
10. Lally, P., van Jaarsveld, C. H. M., Potts, H. W. W., & Wardle, J. (2010). How are habits formed: Modelling habit formation in the real world. *European Journal of Social Psychology, 40*(6), 998-1009.

Chapter 2: Regaining Conscious Control

1. Kandel, E. R., Schwartz, J. H., Jessell, T. M., Siegelbaum, S. A., & Hudspeth, A. J. (2013). *Principles of Neural Science* (5th ed.). McGraw-Hill Education.
2. Miller, E. K., & Cohen, J. D. (2001). An integrative theory of prefrontal cortex function. *Annual Review of Neuroscience, 24,* 167-202.
3. MacLean, P. D. (1990). *The Triune Brain in Evolution: Role in Paleocerebral Functions.* Plenum Press.
4. Teicher, M. H., Anderson, C. M., & Polcari, A. (2012). Childhood maltreatment is associated with reduced volume in the prefrontal cortex and amygdala. *Proceedings of the National Academy of Sciences, 109*(9), E563-E572.
5. Fox, G. R., Kaplan, J., Damasio, H., & Damasio, A. (2015). Neural correlates of gratitude. *Frontiers in Psychology, 6,* 1491.
6. Garland, E. L., & Fredrickson, B. L. (2019). Positive reappraisal and the neurobiology of resilience to stress: From the cognitive model to brain plasticity. *Current Opinion in Psychiatry, 32*(5), 381-386.

Chapter 3: Building a Formidable Soul

1. Kashdan, T. B., & McKnight, P. E. (2013). Commitment to a purpose in life: An antidote to the suffering by individuals with social anxiety disorder. *Emotion, 13*(6), 1150-1159.
2. Siegel, D. J. (2012). *The Developing Mind: How Relationships and the Brain Interact to Shape Who We Are* (2nd ed.). Guilford Press.

3. LeDoux, J. E., & Pine, D. S. (2016). Using neuroscience to help understand fear and anxiety: A two-system framework. *American Journal of Psychiatry, 173*(11), 1083-1093.
4. Barrett, L. F. (2017). *How Emotions Are Made: The Secret Life of the Brain*. Houghton Mifflin Harcourt.
5. Beck, A. T., & Haigh, E. A. P. (2014). Advances in cognitive theory and therapy: The generic cognitive model. *Annual Review of Clinical Psychology, 10*, 1-24.
6. Gross, J. J. (2002). Emotion regulation: Affective, cognitive, and social consequences. *Psychophysiology, 39*(3), 281-291.
7. Davidson, R. J., Putnam, K. M., & Larson, C. L. (2000). Dysfunction in the neural circuitry of emotion regulation: A possible prelude to violence. *Science, 289*(5479), 591-594.
8. Sapolsky, R. M. (2004). Why zebras don't get ulcers: The acclaimed guide to stress, stress-related diseases, and coping. *Nature Reviews Neuroscience, 5*(12), 1071-1072.
9. van der Kolk, B. A. (2014). *The Body Keeps the Score: Brain, Mind, and Body in the Healing of Trauma*. Viking.
10. Porges, S. W. (2011). *The Polyvagal Theory: Neurophysiological Foundations of Emotions, Attachment, Communication, and Self-Regulation*. Norton & Company.
11. Price, C. J., & Hooven, C. (2018). Interoceptive Awareness Skills for Emotion Regulation: Theory and Approach of Mindful Awareness in Body-oriented Therapy (MABT). *Frontiers in Psychology, 9*, 798.
12. Kahneman, D., & Tversky, A. (1979). Prospect theory: An analysis of decision under risk. *Econometrica, 47*(2), 263-291.
13. LeDoux, J. (1996). *The Emotional Brain: The Mysterious Underpinnings of Emotional Life*. Simon & Schuster.

14. Huberman, A. D., & Patapoutian, A. (2021). Physiology and neurobiology of breathing in sleep, stress, and emotional states. *Annual Review of Neuroscience, 44*, 275-297.
15. Arnsten, A. F. T. (2009). Stress signaling pathways that impair prefrontal cortex structure and function. *Nature Reviews Neuroscience, 10*(6), 410-422.
16. Miller, E. K., & Cohen, J. D. (2001). An integrative theory of prefrontal cortex function. *Annual Review of Neuroscience, 24*, 167-202.
17. Schwartz, J. M., & Begley, S. (2002). *The Mind and the Brain: Neuroplasticity and the Power of Mental Force*. HarperCollins.
18. Porges, S. W. (2011). *The Polyvagal Theory: Neurophysiological Foundations of Emotions, Attachment, Communication, and Self-Regulation*. Norton & Company.
19. Arnsten, A. F. T. (2009). Stress signaling pathways that impair prefrontal cortex structure and function. *Nature Reviews Neuroscience, 10*(6), 410-422.
20. Haber, S. N., & Knutson, B. (2010). The Reward Circuit: Linking Primate Anatomy and Human Imaging. *Neuropsychopharmacology, 35*(1), 4-26.
21. Schwartz, J. M., Stapp, H. P., & Beauregard, M. (2005). Quantum physics in neuroscience and psychology: A neurophysical model of mind-brain interaction. *Philosophical Transactions of the Royal Society B: Biological Sciences, 360*(1458), 1309-1327.
22. Pennebaker, J. W., & Smyth, J. M. (2016). *Opening Up by Writing It Down: How Expressive Writing Improves Health and Eases Emotional Pain* (3rd ed.). The Guilford Press.
23. Lieberman, M. D., Eisenberger, N. I., Crockett, M. J., Tom, S. M., Pfeifer, J. H., & Way, B. M. (2007). Putting feelings into words:

Affect labeling disrupts amygdala activity in response to affective stimuli. *Psychological Science*, 18(5), 421-428.
24. Pennebaker, J. W. (1997). Writing about emotional experiences as a therapeutic process. *Psychological Science*, 8(3), 162-166.
25. Nolen-Hoeksema, S., Wisco, B. E., & Lyubomirsky, S. (2008). Rethinking rumination. *Perspectives on Psychological Science*, 3(5), 400-424.
26. Tang, Y. Y., Hölzel, B. K., & Posner, M. I. (2015). The neuroscience of mindfulness meditation: How the body and mind work together. *Nature Reviews Neuroscience*, 16(4), 213-225.
27. Ryff, C. D., & Singer, B. (1998). The contours of positive human health. *Psychological Inquiry*, 9(1), 1-28.
28. Deci, E. L., & Ryan, R. M. (2000). The "what" and "why" of goal pursuits: Human needs and the self-determination of behavior. *Psychological Inquiry*, 11(4), 227-268.
29. Forgeard, M. J. C., & Elstein, J. G. (2014). Advancing the clinical science of creativity. *Frontiers in Psychology*, 5, 613.

Chapter 4: Conquering Inner Chaos

1. Sweeton, J. (2021). *Research and education supporting neuroplasticity and emotional regulation*. Clinical Psychology Review.
2. Sweeton, J. (2021). *The Neuroscience of Trauma: Why Your Brain Feels Broken and What You Can Do About It*. The Trauma Therapist Newsletter.
3. McEwen, B. S. (2006). Protective and damaging effects of stress mediators: Central role of the brain. *Dialogues in Clinical Neuroscience*, 8(4), 367-381.
4. Craig, A. D. (2002). How do you feel? Interoception: The sense of the physiological condition of the body. *Nature Reviews Neuroscience*, 3(8), 655-666.

5. Arnsten, A. F. T. (2009). Stress signaling pathways that impair prefrontal cortex structure and function. *Nature Reviews Neuroscience*, 10(6), 410-422.
6. Etkin, A., Egner, T., & Kalisch, R. (2011). Emotional processing in anterior cingulate and medial prefrontal cortex. *Trends in Cognitive Sciences*, 15(2), 85-93.
7. Beck, A. T. (1995). *Cognitive Therapy: Basics and Beyond*. Guilford Press.
8. van der Kolk, B. A. (2015). *The Body Keeps the Score: Brain, Mind, and Body in the Healing of Trauma*. Penguin Books.
9. Siegel, D. J. (2012). *The Developing Mind: How Relationships and the Brain Interact to Shape Who We Are* (2nd ed.). Guilford Press.
10. Csikszentmihalyi, M. (1996). *Creativity: Flow and the Psychology of Discovery and Invention*. HarperCollins.
11. Gladwell, M. (2008). *Outliers: The Story of Success*. Little, Brown, and Company.
12. Koelsch, S. (2014). *Brain and Body in Music Therapy: The Neuroscience of Music in Mental Health and Disease*. Music Perception: An Interdisciplinary Journal, 31(4), 307-323.
13. Thaut, M. H., McIntosh, G. C., & Hoemberg, V. (2015). Neurobiological foundations of neurologic music therapy: Rhythmic entrainment and the motor system. *Frontiers in Psychology*, 6, 1185.
14. Koenig, J., & Bradt, J. (2017). Music therapy in medical settings. In *Oxford Textbook of Creative Arts, Health, and Wellbeing* (pp. 55-64). Oxford University Press.
15. Thaut, M. H. (2005). *Rhythm, Music, and the Brain: Scientific Foundations and Clinical Applications*. Routledge.
16. Zatorre, R. J., Chen, J. L., & Penhune, V. B. (2007). When the brain plays music: Auditory–motor interactions in music perception and production. *Nature Reviews Neuroscience*, 8(7), 547-558.

17. Levitin, D. J. (2006). *This Is Your Brain on Music: The Science of a Human Obsession*. Dutton/Penguin.
18. Thaut, M. H., & Hoemberg, V. (2014). *Handbook of Neurologic Music Therapy*. Oxford University Press.
19. Altenmüller, E., & Schlaug, G. (2015). Apollo's Gift: New Aspects of Neurologic Music Therapy. *Progress in Brain Research*, 217, 237-252.
20. Bittman, B. B., Berk, L. S., Shannon, M., Sharaf, M., Westengard, J., Guegler, K. J., & Ruff, D. W. (2001). Recreational music-making: A cost-effective group interdisciplinary strategy for reducing burnout and improving mood states in long-term care workers. *Advances in Mind–Body Medicine*, 17(4), 58-67.
21. Friedman, R. L. (2000). *The Healing Power of the Drum: A Psychotherapist Explores the Healing Power of Rhythm*. White Cliffs Media.
22. Koelsch, S. (2010). Towards a neural basis of music-evoked emotions. *Trends in Cognitive Sciences*, 14(3), 131-137.
23. Fancourt, D., & Perkins, R. (2018). Effect of group drumming interventions on anxiety, depression, social resilience, and inflammatory immune response among mental health service users: A randomized control trial. *PLOS ONE*, 13(3), e0193711.

Chapter 5: Creating Your Future Identity

1. Merzenich, M. M. (2013). *Soft-Wired: How the New Science of Brain Plasticity Can Change Your Life*. Parnassus Publishing.
2. Kays, J. L., Hurley, R. A., & Taber, K. H. (2012). The dynamic brain: Neuroplasticity and mental health. *The Journal of Neuropsychiatry and Clinical Neurosciences*, 24(2), 118-124.
3. Siegel, D. J. (2012). *The Developing Mind: How Relationships and the Brain Interact to Shape Who We Are* (2nd ed.). Guilford Press.

4. Oyserman, D., Fryberg, S. A., & Yoder, N. (2007). Identity-based motivation and health. *Journal of Personality and Social Psychology*, 93(6), 1011-1027.
5. Pascual-Leone, A., Amedi, A., Fregni, F., & Merabet, L. B. (2005). The plastic human brain cortex. *Annual Review of Neuroscience*, 28, 377-401.
6. Draganski, B., Gaser, C., Busch, V., Schuierer, G., Bogdahn, U., & May, A. (2004). Changes in grey matter induced by training: Newly honed juggling skills show up as a transient feature on a brain-imaging scan. *Nature*, 427(6972), 311-312.
7. Hebb, D. O. (1949). *The organization of behavior: A neuropsychological theory*. Wiley.
8. Huttenlocher, P. R. (1979). Synaptic density in human frontal cortex: Developmental changes and effects of aging. *Brain Research*, 163(2), 195-205.
9. Damasio, A. R. (1999). *The Feeling of What Happens: Body and Emotion in the Making of Consciousness*. Harcourt Brace.
10. Deci, E. L., & Ryan, R. M. (2000). The "what" and "why" of goal pursuits: Human needs and the self-determination of behavior. *Psychological Inquiry*, 11(4), 227-268.

Chapter 6: Bulletproofing Your Values

1. Chavez, R. S., & Heatherton, T. F. (2017). Representational similarity of social and valence information in the medial prefrontal cortex. *Journal of Cognitive Neuroscience*, 29(5), 755-766.
2. Festinger, L. (1957). *A Theory of Cognitive Dissonance*. Stanford University Press.
3. Rokeach, M. (1973). *The Nature of Human Values*. Free Press.
4. Schwartz, J. M., Stapp, H. P., & Beauregard, M. (2005). Quantum physics in neuroscience and psychology: A neurophysical model of

mind–brain interaction. *Philosophical Transactions of the Royal Society B: Biological Sciences*, 360(1458), 1309-1327.
5. Porges, S. W. (2011). *The Polyvagal Theory: Neurophysiological Foundations of Emotions, Attachment, Communication, and Self-Regulation*. W. W. Norton & Company.

Chapter 7: Slaying Your Goals

1. Heatherton, T. F., & Wagner, D. D. (2011). Cognitive neuroscience of self-regulation failure. *Trends in Cognitive Sciences*, 15(3), 132-139.
2. Locke, E. A., & Latham, G. P. (2002). Building a practically useful theory of goal setting and task motivation: A 35-year odyssey. *American Psychologist*, 57(9), 705-717.
3. Baumeister, R. F., Bratslavsky, E., Finkenauer, C., & Vohs, K. D. (2001). Bad is stronger than good. *Review of General Psychology*, 5(4), 323-370.
4. LeDoux, J. E. (2015). *Anxious: Using the Brain to Understand and Treat Fear and Anxiety*. Viking.
5. Inagaki, T. K., & Eisenberger, N. I. (2012). Neural correlates of giving support to a loved one: A functional magnetic resonance imaging study. *Psychological Science*, 23(9), 1049-1057.
6. Siegel, D. J. (2007). *The Mindful Brain: Reflection and Attunement in the Cultivation of Well-Being*. W. W. Norton & Company.
7. Festinger, L. (1957). *A Theory of Cognitive Dissonance*. Stanford University Press.
8. Miller, E. K., & Cohen, J. D. (2001). An integrative theory of prefrontal cortex function. *Annual Review of Neuroscience*, 24(1), 167-202.
9. Inagaki, T. K., & Eisenberger, N. I. (2012). Neural correlates of giving support to a loved one: A functional magnetic resonance imaging study. *Psychological Science*, 23(9), 1049-1057.

10. Fehr, E., & Camerer, C. F. (2007). Social neuroeconomics: The neural circuitry of social preferences. *Trends in Cognitive Sciences*, 11(10), 419-427.
11. Raz, A., & Buhle, J. (2006). Typologies of attentional networks. *Nature Reviews Neuroscience*, 7(5), 367-379.
12. Ochsner, K. N., & Gross, J. J. (2005). The cognitive control of emotion. *Trends in Cognitive Sciences*, 9(5), 242-249.
13. Raichle, M. E. (2015). The brain's default mode network. *Annual Review of Neuroscience*, 38, 433-447.
14. Lally, P., van Jaarsveld, C. H. M., Potts, H. W. W., & Wardle, J. (2010). How are habits formed: Modeling habit formation in the real world. *European Journal of Social Psychology*, 40(6), 998-1009.
15. McGregor, I., & Little, B. R. (1998). Personal projects, happiness, and meaning: On doing well and being yourself. *Journal of Personality and Social Psychology*, 74(2), 494512.
16. Schultz, W. (2015). Neuronal reward and decision signals: From theories to data. *Physiological Reviews*, 95(3), 853-951.
17. Arnsten, A. F. T. (2009). Stress signalling pathways that impair prefrontal cortex structure and function. *Nature Reviews Neuroscience*, 10(6), 410-422.

Chapter 8. Becoming the B.O.S.S.

1. LeDoux, J. E. (2012). *The Survival Brain: How Our Minds Evolved to Protect Us from Danger and Why It Leads to Anxiety and Fear*. Viking.
2. Miller, E. K., & Cohen, J. D. (2001). An integrative theory of prefrontal cortex function. *Annual Review of Neuroscience*, 24(1), 167-202.
3. Raz, A., & Buhle, J. (2006). Typologies of attentional networks. *Nature Reviews Neuroscience*, 7(5), 367-379.

4. Schwartz, J. M., & Begley, S. (2002). *The Mind and the Brain: Neuroplasticity and the Power of Mental Force.* HarperCollins.

Chapter 9: Dominating Your Results Tracker

1. Matthews, G. (2015). Goal setting and achievement: How writing down goals increases commitment and success. *Journal of Applied Psychology*, 100(6), 1764-1773.
2. Emmons, R. A., & McCullough, M. E. (2003). Counting blessings versus burdens: An experimental investigation of gratitude and subjective well-being in daily life. *Journal of Personality and Social Psychology*, 84(2), 377-389.
3. Schultz, W. (2015). Neuronal reward and decision signals: From theories to data. *Physiological Reviews*, 95(3), 853-951.
4. Doidge, N. (2007). *The Brain That Changes Itself: Stories of Personal Triumph from the Frontiers of Brain Science.* Penguin Books.
5. Sweller, J. (1988). Cognitive load during problem-solving: Effects on learning. *Cognitive Science*, 12(2), 257-285.
6. Miller, E. K., & Cohen, J. D. (2001). An integrative theory of prefrontal cortex function. *Annual Review of Neuroscience*, 24, 167-202.
7. Kounios, J., & Beeman, M. (2009). The Eureka Factor: A Neurocognitive Theory of Insight. *Current Directions in Psychological Science*, 18(4), 210-216.
8. Jung, R. E., & Haier, R. J. (2007). The Parieto-Frontal Integration Theory (P-FIT) of intelligence: Converging neuroimaging evidence. *Behavioral and Brain Sciences*, 30(2), 135-154.
9. Schultz, W. (2016). Dopamine reward prediction-error signaling: A two-component response. *Nature Reviews Neuroscience*, 17(3), 183-195.

10. Panksepp, J., & Biven, L. (2012). *The Archaeology of Mind: Neuroevolutionary Origins of Human Emotions.* W.W. Norton & Company.
11. Choi, K. W., & Langer, E. J. (2017). Joyful Activities and Their Implications for Emotional Well-Being. *Journal of Positive Psychology*, 12(5), 405-414.
12. Dunbar, R. I. M., & Shultz, S. (2017). Evolution in the social brain. *Science*, 317(5843), 1344-1347.
13. Baumeister, R. F., & Leary, M. R. (1995). The Need to Belong: Desire for Interpersonal Attachments as a Fundamental Human Motivation. *Psychological Bulletin*, 117(3), 497-529.
14. Porges, S. W. (2011). *The Polyvagal Theory: Neurophysiological Foundations of Emotions, Attachment, Communication, and Self-Regulation.* Norton Series on Interpersonal Neurobiology.
15. Gross, J. J. (2014). Emotion Regulation: Conceptual and Empirical Foundations. *Handbook of Emotion Regulation*, 3-20.
16. Hölzel, B. K., Carmody, J., Vangel, M., & others. (2011). Mindfulness practice leads to increases in regional brain gray matter density. *Psychiatry Research: Neuroimaging*, 191(1), 36-43.
17. Ratey, J. J., & Hagerman, E. (2008). *Spark: The Revolutionary New Science of Exercise and the Brain.* Little, Brown and Company.
18. Kabat-Zinn, J. (2013). *Full Catastrophe Living: Using the Wisdom of Your Body and Mind to Face Stress, Pain, and Illness.* Bantam Books.
19. Koelsch, S. (2014). *Brain and Music.* Wiley-Blackwell.
20. Lynn-Seraphine, P. (in press). *Neuro-Rhythmic Trauma Therapy: A Qualitative Study.*
21. Lynn-Seraphine, P. (2016). *Neurodrumming: Towards an Integral Mental Fitness Training for Healthy Aging.* Retrieved from http://doi.org/10.13140/RG.2.2.28555.28966

22. Roskies, A. L. (2008). Neuroscientific Perspectives on Decision-Making and Uncertainty. *Journal of Cognitive Neuroscience*, 20(2), 1-15.
23. Gazzaniga, M. S., & Mangun, G. R. (2018). *Cognitive Neuroscience: The Biology of the Mind.* W.W. Norton & Company.

Chapter 10: Firing on all Cylinders
Websites: www.DrPamelaSeraphine.com
& www.HopeAfterTrauma.ca

www.ingramcontent.com/pod-product-compliance
Lightning Source LLC
Chambersburg PA
CBHW030247010526
44107CB00031B/1355/J